TAKEAWAY

NOODLE SOUPS, SALADS AND STIR-FRIES

LES HUYNH

MURDOCH BOOKS

CONTENTS

Takeaway is fresh, fast and healthy Asian food-to-go. There's no need to dash out to your nearest noodle bar, because these simple, fresh recipes can be prepared quickly and easily in the comfort of your own home. These recipes are my own versions of traditional Asian recipes. They all feature noodles—a wonderfully diverse ingredient—which I've used in soups, salads and stir-fries. You'll find most of the things you need in your local Asian grocery store but don't be afraid to improvise if you can't find the exact ingredient—cooking isn't just about following recipes to the letter, it's about creativity and passion. Food that has been prepared with care and food that looks and smells delicious will also tantalize the taste buds. All the recipes in this book can either be eaten as a main meal, or combined with one or more other recipes to be served as part of an Asian banquet. If a recipe serves two to four people (or four to six people, and so on), it will serve two people as a main meal, or four if the dish is part of a banquet.

01**SOUP**RECIPES

In Asia, soups are eaten throughout the day and enjoyed no matter what the season. I remember as a child in Vietnam hungrily slurping a steaming bowl of pho beef soup for breakfast—even in the height of a sweltering summer. This fragrant soup was a favourite, brimming with thin slices of beef and rice noodles and topped with fresh aromatic herbs, so typical of Vietnamese cuisine. Many of the soups in this chapter are based on the traditional soups I enjoyed in Vietnam, while others were inspired by Chinese, Malaysian and Thai soup styles. Most are meals in themselves, such as the rich, coconut-based chicken laksa, while others are lighter and use clear but intensely flavoursome stocks, some of which have a comforting, restorative feel to them. Noodles such as fresh rice noodles, egg or hokkien noodles are added to provide texture, while others such as rice or mung bean vermicelli are used more for their ability to absorb the flavours of the stock. I love making soups on the weekend when I can relax and take my time preparing the stock. The stock, after all, is the most important part of the soup.

BASICS

chicken stock

2 kg (4 lb 8 oz) **chicken carcasses**
2 slices of **fresh ginger**
2 **spring onions (scallions)**, roughly chopped

Remove any fat from the chicken carcasses and clean under cold water. Put all the ingredients into a stockpot or large saucepan with 3 litres (105 fl oz/12 cups) water. Bring to the boil, then reduce the heat and simmer gently. Skim off any scum and fat that rise to the surface during cooking.

Simmer the stock gently for 2–2½ hours. Cool for about 10 minutes, then strain the stock through a fine sieve and discard any solids. Store the stock in the refrigerator for up to 3 days or freeze in small portions for up to 6 months.

Makes about 2.5 litres (87 fl oz/10 cups)

tamarind water

150 g (5½ oz) **seedless tamarind pulp**
300 ml (10½ fl oz) **hot water**

Cover the tamarind pulp with the hot water and leave to soak for 15–20 minutes. Squeeze and work the pulp to dissolve it. Strain the liquid through a sieve and discard the fibre. Store in an airtight container in the refrigerator for up to 5 days.

Makes about 250 ml (9 fl oz/1 cup)

sambal oelek

120 g (4¼ oz) **long red chillies**, roughly chopped
1 tablespoon **sugar**
1 tablespoon **white vinegar**
1 teaspoon **salt**
2 tablespoons **vegetable oil**

Put the chillies in a saucepan and pour in enough water to just cover. Bring to the boil, then reduce the heat and simmer for 5 minutes, or until the chillies soften. Allow to cool, then drain.

Combine the chillies and remaining ingredients in a small food processor and blend to a paste. Store in a tightly sealed jar for up to 1 week or freeze leftover paste in ice cube trays.
Makes about 150 g (5½ oz)

fried shallots

16–20 **red Asian shallots**, thinly sliced
vegetable oil, for deep-frying

Fill a wok or deep-fat fryer one-third full of oil and heat to 160°C (315°F), or until a cube of bread dropped into the oil browns in 30–35 seconds. Carefully add the shallots, standing back as the oil may splash and bubble up. Deep-fry, stirring occasionally, for 1 minute, or until the shallots are crisp. Remove with a slotted spoon and drain on crumpled paper towels. Store the fried shallots for 2 days in an airtight container.
Makes 100 g (3½ oz/ 1 cup)

sichuan beef noodle soup
serves six to eight

3 **garlic cloves**, peeled
1 **lemon grass stem**, white part only, sliced
2 **long red chillies**, seeded and thinly sliced
1½ teaspoons **sichuan peppercorns**, dry-fried
2 teaspoons **coriander seeds**, dry-fried
pinch of **salt**
4 x 150 g (5½ oz) **beef rump steaks**
2 tablespoons **vegetable oil**
500 g (1 lb 2 oz) **hokkien (egg) noodles**

STOCK
2 litres (70 fl oz/8 cups) **beef stock**
1 tablespoon finely grated **fresh ginger**
2 tablespoons **kecap manis**
2 tablespoons **light soy sauce**
2 teaspoons **Chinese black vinegar**
1 teaspoon **sugar**
1 tablespoon **sesame oil**
1 teaspoon **chilli oil** (page 71)

TO SERVE
1 handful **bean sprouts**, trimmed
2 **spring onions (scallions)**, sliced on
  the diagonal
1 handful **coriander (cilantro) leaves**

Using a mortar and pestle, pound the garlic, lemon grass, chilli, peppercorns, coriander seeds and salt to form a fine paste. Put the beef steaks in a bowl and rub with the paste. Leave to marinate in the refrigerator for at least 4 hours, or preferably overnight.

Heat the oil in a chargrill pan over medium heat. Add the beef steaks and chargrill for 2–3 minutes on each side, or until cooked to your liking. Rest in a warm place for 5 minutes. Slice the beef thinly, then cover and keep warm.

To make the stock, combine all the ingredients in a saucepan and bring to the boil. Reduce the heat to a simmer, then season with salt, to taste.

Pour hot water over the hokkien noodles to soften them, then drain. To serve, divide the noodles between individual bowls. Top with the sliced beef and bean sprouts. Ladle the soup over the top and sprinkle with spring onion and coriander.

pho beef soup
serves six to eight

1.5 kg (3 lb 5 oz) **oxtail**, chopped
1.5 kg (3 lb 5 oz) **beef brisket**
10 cm (4 inch) piece **fresh ginger**, unpeeled, bruised
2 **onions**, unpeeled
7 **star anise**
2 **cinnamon sticks**
8 **cloves**
2 **cardamom pods**
3 tablespoons **fish sauce**
1 tablespoon **sugar**
1 teaspoon **salt**
900 g (2 lb) **fresh rice noodles**, 1 cm (1/2 inch) wide
300 g (10 1/2 oz) **beef fillet** or **silverside**, very thinly sliced

TO SERVE
2 large handfuls **bean sprouts**, trimmed
4 **spring onions (scallions)**, thinly sliced
2 handfuls **mixed herbs**, such as Thai basil and coriander (cilantro) leaves
lime wedges

Fill a stockpot or large saucepan three-quarters full with water and bring to the boil. Add the oxtail and brisket and boil for 3–4 minutes, then drain. Rinse the meat. Put 5 litres (175 fl oz/20 cups) water into the cleaned stockpot. Return the oxtail and brisket to the pot and bring to the boil.

Preheat a chargrill pan or barbecue hotplate over medium–high heat. Cook the ginger and whole onions until brown all over to give them a smoky, slightly charred flavour. Add the ginger and onions to the stockpot along with the star anise, cinnamon sticks, cloves and cardamom pods. Bring the stock to the boil, then reduce the heat to a gentle simmer. Cook for 2 hours, then remove the brisket from the stock. Allow the brisket to cool, then slice thinly and set aside.

Continue to simmer the stock for another 1 hour, occasionally skimming the fat from the surface. Strain the stock through a sieve and discard the oxtail, ginger, onions and spices. Return the stock to the cleaned pot and add the fish sauce, sugar and salt. Bring to a gentle simmer.

Pour boiling water over the rice noodles to soften, then drain. To serve, divide the noodles among serving bowls and top with the slices of raw beef fillet or silverside and the slices of brisket. Pour on the hot stock and garnish with bean sprouts, spring onion and herbs. Serve lime wedges on the side for squeezing over the soup.

crabmeat bean vermicelli soup
serves four to six

130 g (4½ oz) **bean thread vermicelli (glass) noodles**
2 tablespoons **oil**
1 **garlic clove**, finely chopped
½ **onion**, finely chopped
2.5 litres (87 fl oz/10 cups) **chicken stock** (page 14)
2 tablespoons **tomato paste (concentrated purée)**
200 g (7 oz) **cooked crabmeat**
2 tablespoons **fish sauce**
1 teaspoon **sugar**
1½ teaspoons **salt**
½ teaspoon **freshly ground black pepper**
2 tablespoons **cornflour (cornstarch)**
1 **egg**, lightly beaten

TO SERVE
1 handful **bean sprouts**, trimmed
2 **spring onions (scallions)**, thinly sliced
1 small handful **coriander (cilantro) leaves**, chopped
sambal oelek (page 15) or **ground chillies** (optional)

Soak the vermicelli noodles in hot water for 5 minutes, then drain well. Cut the noodles into shorter lengths using scissors.

Heat the oil in a large saucepan and fry the garlic and onion until fragrant, then add the stock and tomato paste. Bring to the boil, then reduce the heat to a simmer. Add the crabmeat, fish sauce, sugar, salt and pepper. Dissolve the cornflour in 4 tablespoons water. Slowly pour the cornflour mixture into the stock, stirring constantly until the soup thickens slightly, then pour in the beaten egg in a slow stream. Stir until the egg sets. Check the seasoning.

To serve, divide the noodles among serving bowls and top with bean sprouts. Ladle the hot stock over and garnish with spring onion and coriander. Serve a small bowl of sambal oelek or ground chillies on the side if liked, and add a small amount to the soup to add a bit of bite.

malaysian prawn noodle soup
serves four to six

600 g (1 lb 5 oz) **raw prawns (shrimp)**
300 g (10½ oz) **hokkien (egg) noodles**

STOCK
3 tablespoons **oil**
2 **onions**, sliced
5 **garlic cloves**, crushed
3 tablespoons **dried shrimp**
2 **dried long red chillies**
2 litres (70 fl oz/8 cups) **chicken stock** (page 14)
3 tablespoons **kecap manis**
pinch of **white pepper**

TO SERVE
1 handful **bean sprouts**, trimmed and blanched
2 **spring onions (scallions)**, thinly sliced
3 tablespoons **fried shallots** (page 15)
pinch of **chilli powder**

Peel and devein the prawns, leaving the tails intact and reserving the heads and shells for the stock. Put the prawns in the refrigerator while cooking the stock.

To make the stock, heat the oil in a stockpot or large saucepan. Add the onion, garlic, dried shrimp, chillies and prawn heads and shells and cook for 4–5 minutes, or until fragrant. Use a wooden spoon to crush the prawn heads and shells to release their flavour. Add the chicken stock, kecap manis and white pepper. Simmer to reduce the stock by one-third, then strain. Return the stock to the cleaned stockpot, add salt to taste and bring to the boil. Add the prawns and cook for 3–4 minutes, or until cooked.

Pour hot water over the hokkien noodles to soften them, then drain. Place the noodles into serving bowls and top with the blanched bean sprouts. Ladle the prawns and stock over the noodles. Sprinkle with the spring onion, fried shallots and chilli powder.

bean vermicelli soup with pork meatballs

serves four to six

4 **dried shiitake mushrooms**
8 pieces **dried black fungus**
80 g (2¾ oz) **bean thread vermicelli (glass) noodles**
400 g (14 oz) **minced (ground) pork**
1 small handful **coriander (cilantro) leaves and stems**, finely chopped
4 **spring onions (scallions)**, white part only, finely chopped
½ teaspoon **salt**
pinch of **freshly ground black pepper**
3 tablespoons **vegetable oil**
4 **garlic cloves**, finely chopped
1.5 litres (52 fl oz/6 cups) **chicken stock** (page 14)
2 tablespoons finely chopped **preserved radish**
1 teaspoon **sugar**
1 teaspoon **Chinese black vinegar**
4 tablespoons **light soy sauce**

TO SERVE
1 small handful **coriander (cilantro) leaves**

Soak the mushrooms and fungus in hot water for 10 minutes, or until softened. Drain and discard the stems from the mushrooms and thinly slice the caps. Cut the fungus into small pieces. Soak the vermicelli noodles in hot water for 5 minutes, then drain. Cut the noodles into shorter lengths using scissors.

Combine the pork, coriander leaves and stems, spring onion, salt and pepper in a bowl and mix well. Wet your hands and shape the mixture into small balls, about 1 cm (½ inch) in diameter.

Heat the oil in a small wok or frying pan over low heat, add the garlic and stir-fry until light golden. Remove the wok from the heat. Using a slotted spoon, remove the fried garlic from the oil and drain on paper towels. Reserve the garlic-flavoured oil.

Bring the stock to the boil in a large saucepan. Add the meatballs and simmer for 4–5 minutes, or until they are cooked. Add the mushrooms, fungus, radish, sugar, vinegar and soy sauce and season with salt and pepper, to taste. Add the noodles to the soup. Ladle the noodle soup and meatballs into bowls and sprinkle with coriander. Combine the fried garlic and garlic oil in a bowl and serve on the side for drizzling into the soup.

soy chicken noodle soup
serves four to six

6 **dried shiitake mushrooms**
1 **soy chicken**
2 tablespoons **vegetable oil**
2 **garlic cloves**, finely chopped
2.5 litres (87 fl oz/10 cups) **chicken stock**
  (page 14)
2 cm (¾ inch) piece **fresh ginger**, julienned
2 tablespoons **light soy sauce**
250 g (9 oz) **fresh thin egg noodles**
70 g (2½ oz) **choy sum**, cut into bite-sized
  pieces

TO SERVE
2 **spring onions (scallions)**, thinly sliced
1 handful **coriander (cilantro) leaves**

Soak the mushrooms in hot water until softened. Drain, discard the stems and thinly slice the caps. Remove the meat from the chicken and slice into strips. Set aside.

Heat the oil in a saucepan over low heat, add the garlic and fry until fragrant. Add the mushrooms, stock, ginger and soy sauce and season with salt and pepper. Bring to the boil, then reduce the heat, add the chicken and simmer for 5 minutes.

Bring a large saucepan of water to the boil and cook the noodles for 1–2 minutes, or until softened. Remove the noodles and refresh under cold water, then drain. Blanch the choy sum in the same water for 1 minute. Refresh under cold water, then drain.

Place the noodles into soup bowls with the choy sum. Ladle the chicken and soup over the noodles, then sprinkle with the spring onion and coriander.

HINT _ Soy chickens are sold in Chinatown barbecue shops.

chicken and rice noodle soup with chinese broccoli

serves four to six

2 tablespoons **vegetable oil**
2 **garlic cloves**, finely chopped
3 **red Asian shallots**, thinly sliced
2 litres (70 fl oz/8 cups) **chicken stock** (page 14)
3 cm (1¼ inch) piece **fresh ginger**, julienned
2 **boneless, skinless chicken breasts**, thinly sliced
70 g (2½ oz) **Chinese broccoli (gai larn)**, cut into bite-sized pieces
300 g (10½ oz) **fresh rice noodles**, 1 cm (½ inch) wide

TO SERVE
2 **spring onions (scallions)**, thinly sliced
fish sauce
bird's eye chillies, thinly sliced

Heat the oil in a large saucepan, add the garlic and shallots and stir-fry until fragrant. Pour in the stock and bring to the boil, then reduce the heat to a simmer. Add the ginger and chicken and season with salt and pepper. Cook for 5 minutes, or until the chicken is cooked through. Add the Chinese broccoli and simmer for a further 3 minutes.

Pour boiling water over the rice noodles to soften, then drain. To serve, place the noodles into serving bowls. Ladle the chicken, Chinese broccoli and soup over the noodles and sprinkle with spring onion. Serve with a small bowl of fish sauce and chilli to add to the soup as desired.

curry laksa
serves four to six

200 g (7 oz) **boneless, skinless chicken thighs**, thinly sliced
500 g (1 lb 2 oz) **raw king prawns (shrimp)**, peeled and deveined, tails left intact
800 ml (28 fl oz) **coconut milk**
1 tablespoon **yellow bean paste**
2 tablespoons **fish sauce**
10 **curry leaves**
3 teaspoons **salt**
1 tablespoon **sugar**
8 **fried tofu puffs**, cut into quarters
250 g (9 oz) **rice vermicelli noodles**

PASTE
8 **dried long red chillies**
2 **onions**, chopped
3 **garlic cloves**, crushed
2 **lemon grass stems**, thinly sliced
vegetable oil
1 teaspoon **shrimp paste**
4 tablespoons **medium curry powder** (preferably Ayam brand)
1 teaspoon **ground turmeric**
1/2 teaspoon **ground cloves**

TO SERVE
2 handfuls **bean sprouts**, trimmed
1 **Lebanese (short) cucumber**, seeded and cut into thin lengths
1 handful **Vietnamese mint**
3 tablespoons **fried shallots** (page 15)
sambal oelek (page 15) or chopped **bird's eye chillies** (optional)
lime wedges

To make the paste, discard the seeds and stems from the dried chillies, then soak in hot water for 10 minutes. Drain, then roughly chop. Put the chilli into a food processor with the onion, garlic and lemon grass and add a little of the oil to help blend the mixture into a smooth paste. Heat 3 tablespoons oil in a saucepan over medium–high heat. Add the paste and stir-fry for about 2 minutes, stirring constantly, until fragrant. Add the remaining paste ingredients and stir-fry for 1–2 minutes.

Toss in the chicken and stir-fry for a further 2 minutes. Add the prawns, 1.5 litres (52 fl oz/6 cups) water, the coconut milk, yellow bean paste, fish sauce and curry leaves and bring to the boil, then reduce to a simmer. Add the salt, sugar and tofu puffs.

Place the vermicelli noodles in a bowl, cover with boiling water and soak for 5–7 minutes, or until softened. Drain well. To serve, put the noodles into individual bowls and top with the bean sprouts and cucumber. Ladle the hot soup over the noodles and sprinkle with mint and fried shallots. Offer a small bowl of sambal oelek or chopped chillies alongside and serve with lime wedges for squeezing over the soup.

roasted duck with shiitake mushrooms and egg noodles serves six to eight

6 **dried shiitake mushrooms**
1 **Chinese roasted duck**
2 tablespoons **vegetable oil**
2 **garlic cloves**, crushed
1/2 teaspoon finely grated **fresh ginger**
1/2 teaspoon **five-spice**
2.5 litres (87 fl oz/10 cups) **chicken stock**
  (page 14)
1 1/2 tablespoons **soy sauce**
1 1/2 tablespoons **fish sauce**
2 teaspoons **sugar**
pinch of **salt**
400 g (14 oz) **fresh thin egg noodles**
3 **baby bok choy (pak choy)**, leaves separated
  and cut diagonally into wide strips

TO SERVE
2 **spring onions (scallions)**, thinly sliced on
  the diagonal
1 handful **coriander (cilantro) leaves**

Soak the mushrooms in hot water until softened. Drain, discard the stems and thinly slice the caps. Remove the skin and meat from the duck and thinly slice. Set aside.

Heat the oil in a large saucepan and fry the garlic, ginger and five-spice until fragrant. Add the mushrooms and stock, bring to the boil, then add the soy sauce, fish sauce, sugar and salt. Reduce the heat and simmer for 10 minutes.

Bring a large saucepan of water to the boil and cook the noodles for 1–2 minutes, or until softened. Remove and refresh under cold water, then drain. Blanch the bok choy in the same water for 30 seconds, then refresh under cold water.

To serve, divide the noodles among serving bowls and lay the bok choy and slices of duck on top of the noodles. Ladle over the soup and sprinkle with spring onion and coriander.

chicken and bean
vermicelli soup
serves four to six

2 tablespoons **vegetable oil**
1 **garlic clove**, finely chopped
2.5 litres (87 fl oz/10 cups) **chicken stock** (page 14)
2 **boneless, skinless chicken breasts**
1 small **daikon**, roughly chopped
1 **carrot**, roughly chopped
8 **peppercorns**
1/2 **onion**, cut into wedges
80 g (2¾ oz) **bean thread vermicelli (glass) noodles**
2 tablespoons **light soy sauce**
1/2 teaspoon **sugar**

TO SERVE
1 handful **bean sprouts**, trimmed
2 **spring onions (scallions)**, thinly sliced
2 tablespoons **fried shallots** (page 15)
1 handful **mixed herbs**, such as Thai basil, sawtooth coriander (cilantro)
and coriander (cilantro) leaves
2 tablespoons chopped **roasted peanuts** (page 70)
fish sauce
bird's eye chillies, thinly sliced
lime wedges

Heat the oil in a small wok or frying pan over low heat, add the garlic and stir-fry until light golden. Remove the wok from the heat. Using a slotted spoon, remove the fried garlic and drain on paper towels. Reserve the garlic-flavoured oil.

Bring the stock to the boil in a stockpot or large saucepan. Carefully lower the chicken into the pot, then add the daikon, carrot, peppercorns and onion. Return the stock to the boil, then reduce the heat and simmer for 10 minutes. Turn off the heat, cover with a lid and leave the chicken to cool in the liquid for 20 minutes—it will continue to cook during this time.

Meanwhile, soak the vermicelli noodles in hot water for 5 minutes, then drain. Cut the noodles into shorter lengths using scissors.

Remove the chicken from the stock, reserving the stock. Allow the chicken to cool completely, then shred the meat and set it aside. Strain the stock and return it to the cleaned pot. Bring the stock to the boil and add the soy sauce, sugar and salt, to taste.

To serve, place the noodles into serving bowls. Top with the chicken, bean sprouts and spring onion, then ladle over the boiling stock. Sprinkle with the fried shallots, mixed herbs and roasted peanuts. Combine the fried garlic and garlic oil in a bowl and drizzle a little into the soup. Combine some fish sauce and sliced chilli in a small bowl and serve alongside the soup. Serve with lime wedges for squeezing over the soup.

braised beef noodles
serves four to six

3 tablespoons **oil**
1 large **onion**, quartered
4 **garlic cloves**, crushed
2 **lemon grass stems**, halved, stems bruised
800 g (1 lb 12 oz) **beef chuck** or **stewing beef**,
    trimmed of sinew and cut into 2 cm (3/4 inch) cubes
2 **carrots**, cut into bite-sized pieces
1 **daikon**, cut into bite-sized pieces
500 g (1 lb 2 oz) **fresh rice noodles**, 1 cm (1/2 inch) wide

BRAISING STOCK
1.25 litres (44 fl oz/5 cups) **chicken stock** (page 14)
5 **star anise**
4 tablespoons **ground (brown) bean sauce**
3 tablespoons **tomato paste (concentrated purée)**
2 tablespoons **medium curry powder**
2 tablespoons **sugar**

TO SERVE
1 handful **bean sprouts**, trimmed
1 handful **Vietnamese mint**, sliced
3 **bird's eye chillies**, thinly sliced
lime wedges

Heat the oil in a large saucepan over medium heat. Add the onion, garlic and lemon grass and fry for 1 minute. Add the beef cubes and stir-fry for 2–3 minutes. Add all the braising stock ingredients, season with salt and bring to the boil. Reduce the heat and simmer gently for 1–1 1/2 hours, or until the beef is almost tender. Add the carrot and daikon and cook until the vegetables are soft.

Pour boiling water over the rice noodles to soften, then drain. To serve, divide the noodles among serving bowls, top with the bean sprouts, then ladle the braised beef soup over the top. Sprinkle with Vietnamese mint. Serve with salt and pepper and a bowl of sliced chillies, accompanied by lime wedges for squeezing over the soup.

chicken curry noodles
serves four to six

6 **dried long red chillies**
pinch of **salt**
2 tablespoons **medium curry powder**
600 g (1 lb 5 oz) **boneless, skinless chicken thighs**, sliced into 1 cm (1/2 inch) strips
on the diagonal
3 tablespoons **vegetable oil**
1 **onion**, halved and cut into thick slices
4 **garlic cloves**, crushed
3 cm (1 1/4 inch) piece **fresh ginger**, finely grated
7–8 **makrut (kaffir lime) leaves**, roughly torn
2 **lemon grass stems**, white part only, bruised
1 litre (35 fl oz/4 cups) **coconut milk**
250 g (9 oz) **rice vermicelli noodles**

TO SERVE
1 handful **bean sprouts**, trimmed
1 handful **Thai basil leaves**, sliced
3 **bird's eye chillies**, finely chopped
lime wedges

Discard the seeds and stems from the dried chillies. Soak in hot water for 10 minutes, then
drain and roughly chop. Using a mortar and pestle, pound the chillies with the salt to form
a paste, then stir in the curry powder. Put the chicken strips in a bowl, add the paste and
mix well to coat. Marinate in the refrigerator for at least 1 hour.

Heat the oil in a saucepan over low–medium heat. Add the onion, garlic and ginger and
stir-fry for 4–5 minutes, or until fragrant. Add the chicken and stir-fry for 4–5 minutes. Add
the makrut leaves, lemon grass and coconut milk and bring to the boil, then reduce the
heat and simmer for 20 minutes, or until the chicken is cooked. Season with salt and
pepper, then cook for a further 5 minutes.

Place the vermicelli noodles in a bowl, cover with boiling water and leave to soak for
5–7 minutes, or until softened. Drain well.

To serve, place the noodles into individual bowls and top with bean sprouts and Thai
basil, then ladle the chicken curry over. Serve accompanied with bowls of chopped
chillies and lime wedges.

char siu noodle soup
serves four to six

3 tablespoons **vegetable oil**
4 **garlic cloves**, finely chopped
2 litres (70 fl oz/8 cups) **chicken stock** (page 14)
5 **makrut (kaffir lime) leaves**
2 tablespoons **fish sauce**
1 tablespoon **sugar**
pinch of **freshly ground black pepper**
pinch of **salt**
180 g (6½ oz) **fresh thin egg noodles**
50 g (1¾ oz/1 cup) thinly sliced **Chinese cabbage (wong bok)**

TO SERVE
1 handful **bean sprouts**, trimmed
300 g (10½ oz) **Chinese barbecued pork (char siu)**, thinly sliced
2 **spring onions (scallions)**, thinly sliced
1 handful **coriander (cilantro) leaves**
1 tablespoon finely chopped **bird's eye chillies**
2 tablespoons ground **roasted peanuts** (page 70)

Heat the oil in a small wok or frying pan over low heat, add the garlic and stir-fry until light golden. Remove the wok from the heat. Using a slotted spoon, remove the fried garlic and drain on paper towels. Reserve the garlic-flavoured oil.

Put the stock in a saucepan and bring to the boil. Add the makrut leaves, fish sauce, sugar, pepper and salt, then lower the heat to a simmer.

Bring a large saucepan of water to the boil and cook the egg noodles for 1–2 minutes, or until softened. Remove and refresh under cold water, then drain. Blanch the Chinese cabbage in the same water for 30 seconds, then drain.

Place the noodles and Chinese cabbage in serving bowls. Top with the bean sprouts and pork and ladle the soup over, then sprinkle with spring onion, coriander, chilli and peanuts. Combine the fried garlic and garlic oil in a small bowl and serve on the side for drizzling into the soup.

long and short soup
serves six

WON TONS
130 g (4½ oz) **minced (ground) pork**
150 g (5½ oz) **raw prawns (shrimp)**, peeled and deveined, finely chopped
½ teaspoon finely grated **fresh ginger**
3 teaspoons **light soy sauce**
3 **spring onions (scallions)**, white part only, thinly sliced
pinch of **white pepper**
pinch of **sugar**
¾ teaspoon **sesame oil**
30 **square won ton skins**
1 small **egg white**, lightly beaten

SOUP
2 litres (70 fl oz/8 cups) **chicken stock** (page 14)
2 tablespoons **light soy sauce**
2 tablespoons **shaoxing rice wine** or **dry sherry**
1 tablespoon **Chinese black vinegar**
2 teaspoons **salt**
½ teaspoon **white pepper**
250 g (9 oz) **fresh thin egg noodles**

TO SERVE
2 **spring onions (scallions)**, thinly sliced
1 handful **coriander (cilantro) leaves**
30 g (1 oz/⅓ small bunch) **garlic chives**, thinly sliced

To make the won tons, put the pork, prawns, ginger, soy sauce, spring onion, white pepper, sugar and sesame oil in a bowl and mix well to combine. Place a teaspoon of the filling in the centre of a won ton skin. Brush the edges with the egg white, then fold over to form a triangle and pinch along the edges to seal. Repeat with the remaining filling and won ton skins.

To make the soup, bring the stock to the boil in a large saucepan and add the soy sauce, rice wine, vinegar, salt and white pepper. Gently drop the won tons into the boiling stock and cook for 4–5 minutes, or until cooked through.

Bring a large saucepan of water to the boil and cook the noodles for 1–2 minutes, or until softened. Remove and refresh under cold water, then drain. To serve, place the noodles into individual bowls. Ladle the won tons and soup over the noodles and sprinkle with spring onion, coriander and garlic chives.

duck dumpling noodle soup
serves six to eight

DUMPLINGS

2 **dried shiitake mushrooms**
1/2 **Chinese roasted duck**
1 **spring onion (scallion)**, thinly sliced
1/2 teaspoon finely grated **fresh ginger**
1/2 tablespoon **oyster sauce**
32 **square won ton skins**

SOUP

2.5 litres (87 fl oz/10 cups) **chicken stock** (page 14)
100 ml (3 1/2 fl oz) **light soy sauce**
1 1/2 tablespoons **oyster sauce**
1 1/2 tablespoons **kecap manis**
pinch of **white pepper**
400 g (14 oz) **fresh rice noodles**, 1 cm (1/2 inch) wide
80 g (2 3/4 oz) **Chinese broccoli (gai larn)**, shredded

TO SERVE

2 **spring onions (scallions)**, thinly sliced
2 tablespoons **fried shallots** (page 15)

To make the dumplings, soak the mushrooms in hot water until softened. Drain and discard the stems and finely chop the caps. Remove the skin and meat from the duck and finely chop. Combine the mushrooms and duck in a bowl. Add the spring onion, ginger and oyster sauce and mix well. Place 1 teaspoon of the filling in the centre of a won ton skin, then gather all the edges together in the centre. Pinch and twist to seal. Repeat with the remaining filling and won ton skins.

To make the soup, put the stock, soy sauce, oyster sauce, kecap manis and white pepper in a saucepan. Season with salt and bring to the boil. Drop the dumplings into the soup and cook for 3–4 minutes, or until the dumplings rise to the surface. Remove the pan from the heat.

Pour boiling water over the noodles to soften, then drain. Blanch the Chinese broccoli in boiling water for 30 seconds. Drain, refresh under cold water, then drain. To serve, place the rice noodles into bowls, top with the Chinese broccoli, then ladle the dumplings and soup over the noodles. Sprinkle with spring onion and fried shallots.

fish ball and noodle soup

serves six to eight

3 tablespoons **vegetable oil**

3 **garlic cloves**, finely chopped

500 g (1 lb 2 oz) **boneless white fish fillets**, skinned and roughly sliced

1 teaspoon **salt**

pinch of **white pepper**

3 tablespoons **cornflour (cornstarch)**

300 g (10½ oz) **rice vermicelli noodles**

2.5 litres (87 fl oz/10 cups) **chicken stock** (page 14)

2 tablespoons **fish sauce**

1½ tablespoons **light soy sauce**

TO SERVE

2 handfuls **bean sprouts**, trimmed

2 **spring onions (scallions)**, finely chopped

1 handful **coriander (cilantro) leaves**

25 g (1 oz/¼ bunch) **garlic chives**, snipped

soy sauce

3 **bird's eye chillies**, thinly sliced

Heat the oil in a small wok or frying pan and stir-fry the garlic until light golden. Remove the wok from the heat. Using a slotted spoon, remove the fried garlic and drain on paper towels. Reserve the garlic-flavoured oil.

Put the fish in a food processor and process to form a paste. Transfer to a bowl, then add the salt, white pepper and cornflour and knead together. Roll the paste into small balls about the size of a walnut. Fill a stockpot or large saucepan with water and bring to the boil. Drop in the fish balls and cook for 3–4 minutes. Drain and refresh under cold water, then drain well.

Put the vermicelli noodles in a bowl, cover with boiling water and leave to soak for 5–7 minutes, or until softened. Drain well. Cut the noodles into shorter lengths using scissors.

Pour the stock into a large saucepan or stockpot, bring to the boil, then reduce the heat to a simmer. Add the fish sauce, soy sauce and fish balls and season with salt, to taste.

Divide the noodles between bowls and top with bean sprouts. Ladle the stock and fish balls over the noodles. Sprinkle with spring onion, coriander and garlic chives. Combine the fried garlic and garlic oil in a small bowl and serve on the side for drizzling into the soup. Serve with soy sauce and sliced chilli to add to the soup as desired.

chicken noodle soup
serves six to eight

2 litres (70 fl oz/8 cups) **chicken stock** (page 14)
2 **boneless, skinless chicken breasts**
1 **celery stalk**, roughly chopped
5 **white peppercorns**
1/2 **onion**, peeled
200 g (7 oz) **bean thread vermicelli (glass) noodles**
1 1/2 tablespoons **fish sauce**
1/2 teaspoon **sugar**
1/2 teaspoon **salt**

TO SERVE
1 large handful **bean sprouts**, trimmed
15 g (1/2 oz) **garlic chives**, cut into 3 cm (1 1/4 inch) lengths
1 handful **coriander (cilantro) leaves**
2 tablespoons **fried shallots** (page 15)
fish sauce

Bring the stock to the boil in a stockpot or large saucepan. Carefully lower the chicken into the pot, then add the celery, peppercorns and onion. Return to the boil, then reduce the heat and simmer gently for 10 minutes. Turn off the heat. Cover the stockpot with a tight lid and leave the chicken to cool in the liquid for 20 minutes—it will continue to cook during this time.

Meanwhile, soak the noodles in hot water for 5 minutes, then drain. Cut the noodles into shorter lengths using scissors.

Lift the chicken out of the stock, reserving the stock. Allow the chicken to cool completely, then shred the meat and set it aside. Strain the stock and return it to the cleaned pot. Bring to the boil and season with the fish sauce, sugar and salt.

To serve, divide the noodles among the serving bowls. Top with the shredded chicken, bean sprouts and garlic chives. Pour on the hot stock, then sprinkle with coriander and fried shallots. Serve with extra fish sauce, to taste.

coconut chicken noodles
serves four

1 litre (35 fl oz/4 cups) **chicken stock** (page 14)
600 ml (21 fl oz) **coconut milk**
2 **lemon grass stems**, bruised
6 **coriander (cilantro) roots**, cleaned
10 **makrut (kaffir lime) leaves**, torn
4 **long red chillies**, seeded and sliced
4 tablespoons **fish sauce**
90 ml (3 fl oz) **lime juice**
1½ teaspoons **sugar**
350 g (12 oz) **boneless, skinless chicken breasts**, thinly sliced
250 g (9 oz) **fresh rice noodles**, 1 cm (½ inch) wide

TO SERVE
1 handful **coriander (cilantro) leaves**
lime wedges

Put the stock, coconut milk, lemon grass, coriander roots, makrut leaves and chilli in a large saucepan. Bring to the boil, then reduce the heat and simmer for 20 minutes. Discard the coriander roots and lemon grass, then season with the fish sauce, lime juice and sugar. Add the chicken and cook for 6–8 minutes, or until the chicken is cooked. Add the noodles and bring to the boil.

Ladle the soup into serving bowls and sprinkle with coriander. Serve with lime wedges for squeezing over the soup. Serve immediately.

pho chicken soup
serves four to six

2 **cinnamon sticks**
1 tablespoon **white peppercorns**
1 **black Asian cardamom pod**, lightly crushed (optional)
2.2 kg (5 lb) **chicken**, cut into 8 pieces
10 cm (4 inch) piece **fresh ginger**, unpeeled, bruised
1 **onion**, peeled
3 tablespoons **fish sauce**
1 tablespoon **sugar**
1 teaspoon **salt**
pinch of **white pepper**
600 g (1 lb 5 oz) **fresh rice noodles**, 1 cm (½ inch) wide

TO SERVE
2 large handfuls **bean sprouts**, trimmed
1 handful **Thai basil leaves**
1 handful **coriander (cilantro) leaves**
1 handful **sawtooth coriander (cilantro) leaves**, sliced (optional)
½ **onion**, thinly sliced
lime wedges
2 small **bird's eye chillies**, finely chopped
4 tablespoons **hoisin sauce**

Heat a heavy-based frying pan over low heat. Add the cinnamon sticks, peppercorns and cardamom pod (if using) and cook, stirring, for 3–4 minutes, or until fragrant. Remove the spices from the pan and allow to cool. Once cool, wrap in a piece of muslin (cheesecloth) and tie securely.

Put 3.5 litres (122 fl oz/14 cups) water into a stockpot or large saucepan. Add the chicken pieces, ginger, onion and spice bag and bring to the boil. Reduce the heat and simmer for 2 hours, skimming off any fat from the surface. Remove the chicken and allow to cool. Using your hands, remove the skin and roughly shred the meat.

Strain the stock, discarding the ginger, onion and spice bag. Return the stock to the cleaned stockpot and bring to the boil. Add the fish sauce, sugar, salt and white pepper and reduce the heat to a simmer.

Pour boiling water over the rice noodles to soften, then drain. To serve, divide the noodles between individual bowls and top with the chicken, bean sprouts, Thai basil, coriander, sawtooth coriander (if using) and onion slices. Ladle the hot stock into the bowls. Serve with separate bowls of lime wedges, chilli and hoisin sauce.

HINT _ Black cardamom pods can be found in most Asian grocery stores.

hot and sour seafood noodles serves four to six

500 g (1 lb 2 oz) **fresh seafood**, such as squid,
    fish fillet and prawns (shrimp), cleaned,
    peeled and cut into bite-sized pieces
2 tablespoons **vegetable oil**
1 **onion**, sliced
2 **garlic cloves**, crushed
2 **lemon grass stems**, white part only, bruised
1.5 litres (52 fl oz/6 cups) **chicken stock**
    (page 14)
2 **celery stalks**, thinly sliced on the diagonal
1 large **tomato**, cut into thin wedges
80 g (2¾ oz/½ cup) **pineapple chunks**
2 tablespoons **fish sauce**
100 ml (3½ fl oz) **tamarind water** (page 14)
1½ tablespoons **sugar**
1 teaspoon **salt**
200 g (7 oz) **rice vermicelli noodles**

MARINADE
2 **long red chillies**, seeded and finely chopped
1 tablespoon **fish sauce**
pinch of **freshly ground black pepper**

TO SERVE
2 handfuls **bean sprouts**, trimmed
1 handful **fresh Asian herbs**, such as paddy
    herbs and sawtooth coriander (cilantro)
    leaves, sliced
1 **spring onion (scallion)**, sliced

Combine the marinade ingredients in a small bowl. Put the seafood pieces in a bowl and coat well with the marinade. Marinate in the refrigerator for 15–20 minutes.

Heat the oil in a saucepan, add the onion, garlic and lemon grass and stir-fry for about 30 seconds, or until fragrant. Add the stock, celery, tomato and pineapple, then season with the fish sauce, tamarind water, sugar and salt. Bring to the boil, then reduce the heat and simmer for 2–3 minutes. Add the seafood and simmer for a further 2–3 minutes, or until the seafood is cooked.

Place the vermicelli noodles in a bowl, cover with boiling water and leave for 5–7 minutes, or until softened. Drain well.

To serve, place the noodles into individual bowls and top with the bean sprouts. Ladle the seafood and stock over and sprinkle with fresh herbs and spring onion.

HINTS _ Paddy herbs are an aromatic herb used in Vietnam to flavour and garnish soups. Sawtooth coriander (cilantro) is named for its long jagged leaves, similar but stronger in flavour and aroma than ordinary coriander. Both herbs are available from most Asian greengrocers.

thai spicy prawn noodles
serves four to six

200 g (7 oz) **rice vermicelli noodles**
3 tablespoons **oil**
4 **garlic cloves**, crushed
2 **long red chillies**, seeded if preferred, thinly sliced
2 **lemon grass stems**, white part only, bruised
8 slices **fresh galangal**
2 litres (70 fl oz/8 cups) **chicken stock** (page 14)
8 **makrut (kaffir lime) leaves**, torn
3 tablespoons **fish sauce**
2 tablespoons **tamarind water** (page 14)
4 tablespoons **lime juice**
1 teaspoon **salt**
2 teaspoons **sugar**
500 g (1 lb 2 oz) **raw prawns (shrimp)**, peeled and deveined, tails left intact

TO SERVE
1 handful **bean sprouts**, trimmed
1 handful **coriander (cilantro) leaves**

Place the vermicelli noodles in a bowl, cover with boiling water and leave to soak for 5–7 minutes, or until softened. Drain well.

Heat the oil in a large saucepan over medium-high heat. Add the garlic, chilli, lemon grass and galangal and fry until fragrant. Add the stock and makrut leaves and bring to the boil. Reduce the heat to a simmer, then add the fish sauce, tamarind water, lime juice, salt and sugar. Add the prawns and simmer for 2–3 minutes, or until the prawns are cooked. To serve, put the noodles into individual bowls and top with bean sprouts. Ladle the prawns and stock over the noodles and sprinkle with coriander.

spicy chicken noodle soup
serves four to six

2.2 kg (5 lb) **chicken**, chopped into 8 pieces
20 **black peppercorns**
1 handful **celery leaves**, roughly chopped
1 **onion**, peeled

FLAVOURINGS
1 tablespoon **vegetable oil**
4 **garlic cloves**, crushed
1 teaspoon grated **fresh ginger**
3 **long red chillies**, seeded and finely chopped
1 **onion**, finely chopped
1 teaspoon **shrimp paste**
1/2 teaspoon **ground turmeric**
1 tablespoon **ground coriander**
1 teaspoon **ground cumin**
1 teaspoon **ground fennel**
8 **makrut (kaffir lime) leaves**, torn
2 tablespoons **yellow bean paste**
2 tablespoons **fish sauce**
2 teaspoons **sugar**
600 g (1 lb 5 oz) **fresh rice noodles**, 1 cm (1/2 inch) wide

TO SERVE
2 **spring onions (scallions)**, thinly sliced on the diagonal
3 tablespoons **fried shallots** (page 15)
1 handful **Thai basil leaves**
lime wedges

Put the chicken pieces into a stockpot or large saucepan with 3 litres (105 fl oz/12 cups) water, the peppercorns, celery leaves and whole onion and season with salt. Bring to the boil, then reduce the heat and simmer for 1½–2 hours, skimming off any fat that rises to the surface. Remove the chicken and cool. Remove the skin and meat, then shred the chicken meat with your hands. Strain the stock and discard the peppercorns, celery and onion.

Heat the oil in a large saucepan over medium–high heat. Add the garlic, ginger, chilli and chopped onion and fry until fragrant. Add the shrimp paste and fry until the shrimp paste is broken up. Add the spices and fry for 1–2 minutes. Pour in the strained stock, then add the makrut leaves, yellow bean paste, fish sauce and sugar. Bring to the boil, then reduce the heat to a simmer. Season with salt, to taste.

Pour boiling water over the rice noodles to soften, then drain. Place the noodles into individual bowls, top with the shredded chicken and ladle over the soup. Sprinkle with spring onion, fried shallots and Thai basil and serve with lime wedges.

pork and prawn noodle soup
serves four to six

20 g (¾ oz) **dried squid** (optional)
2 tablespoons **vegetable oil**
2 **garlic cloves**, crushed
1 large **carrot**, roughly chopped
10 **black peppercorns**
200 g (7 oz) **pork neck fillet**
3 litres (105 fl oz/12 cups) **chicken stock** (page 14)
250 g (9 oz) **dried rice stick noodles**
24 **raw prawns (shrimp)**, peeled and deveined, tails left intact
1 tablespoon **fish sauce**
1 tablespoon **soy sauce**

TO SERVE
1 handful **bean sprouts**, trimmed
2 **spring onions (scallions)**, thinly sliced
1 handful **coriander (cilantro) leaves**
4 **bird's eye chillies**, finely chopped
3 tablespoons **lime juice**
2 tablespoons **fish sauce**

To make the stock, first soak the dried squid (if using) in lukewarm water for 20 minutes, then drain. Heat the oil in a stockpot or large saucepan and fry the garlic until fragrant. Add the squid, carrot, peppercorns and pork fillet and stir. Pour in the chicken stock and bring to the boil, then reduce the heat and simmer for 1 hour, skimming off any fat that rises to the surface during cooking. Remove the pork and allow to cool, then slice thinly.

Soak the noodles in lukewarm water for 15 minutes until softened. Drain and set aside.

Strain the stock, discarding the solids. Return the stock to the cleaned pot, bring to the boil and add the prawns, fish sauce, soy sauce and season with salt, to taste. Simmer for 3–4 minutes, or until the prawns are cooked.

Bring a large saucepan of water to the boil and cook the noodles for 2–3 minutes, or until soft. Place the noodles into individual bowls.

To serve, top the noodles with the pork slices and bean sprouts, then ladle the prawns and stock over. Sprinkle with spring onion and coriander. Combine the chilli, lime juice and fish sauce in a small bowl and serve alongside the soup.

fish noodle soup

serves six to eight

150 g (5½ oz) chopped **choy sum** or **bok choy (pak choy)**
400 g (14 oz) **fresh thin egg noodles**
2 litres (70 fl oz/8 cups) **chicken stock** (page 14)
1 tablespoon **soy sauce**
2 tablespoons **fish sauce**
1 tablespoon **sugar**
1 tablespoon **salt**
pinch of **white pepper**
500 g (1 lb 2 oz) **white fish fillets**, such as ling or perch, skinned and thinly sliced on the diagonal

TO SERVE
1 handful **spring onions (scallions)**, thinly sliced on the diagonal
1 handful **coriander (cilantro) leaves**
2 tablespoons **fried shallots** (page 15)
soy sauce
3 small **bird's eye chillies**, thinly sliced

Bring a large saucepan of salted water to the boil. Add the choy sum and cook for 20 seconds. Remove with a slotted spoon to a sieve, refresh under cold water, then drain. Add the noodles to the boiling water and cook for 1–2 minutes. Refresh under cold water, then drain.

Put the stock in a large saucepan and add the soy sauce, fish sauce, sugar, salt, white pepper and fish. Simmer for about 2 minutes, or until the fish is cooked.

Divide the noodles and choy sum among individual bowls and ladle the stock and fish over. Sprinkle with spring onion, coriander and fried shallots. Combine some soy sauce and chilli in a small bowl and serve with the soup.

02**SALAD**RECIPES

A salad embodies many of the things I really love about Asian food—healthy, fresh flavours, contrasting textures and refreshing, aromatic herbs. A Southeast Asian salad is meant to be eaten as a main meal and doesn't really resemble the leafy green salad that Western palates are most familiar with, eaten as an accompaniment to pasta or a meat dish. The salad recipes in this chapter all feature noodles, to which pork, beef, seafood or vegetables are added, with fresh herbs such as mint, coriander (cilantro) and Thai basil stirred through at the end. Fried shallots, fried garlic, sesame seeds and peanuts add contrast in texture, and I like to toss in bean sprouts, not only for their soft crunchiness but also, like the noodles, to soak up the flavours of the dressing. These salads are served warm or at room temperature, and you can choose from light dishes such as pork salad with glass noodles, mint and ginger, or the more filling grilled chicken noodle salad.

BASICS

roasted sesame seeds

2 tablespoons **sesame seeds** (white or black)

Dry-fry the sesame seeds in a frying pan over low heat, stirring regularly until the seeds swell and are lightly roasted but not burnt. Cool, then store in an airtight container for up to 1 month.
Makes 2 tablespoons

roasted nuts

160 g (5½ oz/1 cup) **unsalted peanuts** or **cashew nuts**

Dry-fry the nuts in a frying pan over low heat, stirring regularly until the nuts are lightly roasted on the outside. Store the roasted nuts in an airtight container in the refrigerator for up to 3 months. Grind or chop as needed.
Makes 160 g (5½ oz/1 cup)

roasted shredded coconut

30 g (1 oz/½ cup) **shredded coconut**

Dry-fry the coconut in a frying pan over medium–low heat, stirring regularly until the coconut swells and is lightly roasted. Cool, then store in an airtight container for up to 1 month.
Makes 30 g (1 oz/½ cup)

nuoc cham

2 **long red chillies**, seeded and roughly chopped
2 **garlic cloves**, peeled
2 tablespoons **caster (superfine) sugar**
2 tablespoons **lime juice**
3 tablespoons **fish sauce**
1 tablespoon **vinegar**

Using a mortar and pestle, pound the chillies and garlic into a paste. Alternatively, chop the ingredients into a paste using a small food processor. Add the sugar, lime juice, fish sauce, vinegar and 2 tablespoons water. Stir until the sugar dissolves. Store in a tightly sealed jar in the refrigerator for up to 1 week.

Makes about 160 ml (5¼ fl oz)

chilli and rice vinegar

100 ml (3½ fl oz) **rice vinegar** or **coconut vinegar**
1 tablespoon **caster (superfine) sugar**
3 small **bird's eye chillies**, finely chopped

Combine all the ingredients in a bowl and stir until the sugar dissolves. Store in a tightly sealed jar in the refrigerator for up to 1 week.

Makes about 125 ml (4 fl oz/½ cup)

chilli oil

250 ml (9 fl oz/1 cup) **vegetable oil**
1 tablespoon **sichuan peppercorns**
4 **dried red chillies**, thinly sliced

Heat the oil in a wok over low heat. Add the peppercorns and chilli and cook for 15 minutes, stirring. Set aside and allow to cool. Once cool, transfer to a lidded jar for 2–3 days to allow the flavour to develop. After this time, strain the oil and discard the peppercorns and chilli. Store the oil in a tightly sealed jar in a cool place for up to 3 months.

Makes 250 ml (9 fl oz/1 cup)

rice paper rolls
serves four

Place the vermicelli noodles in a bowl, cover with boiling water and soak for 5–7 minutes, or until softened. Drain well.

60 g (2¼ oz) **rice vermicelli noodles**
8 **rice paper wrappers**
8 **butter lettuce leaves**
150 g (5½ oz) **ready-to-eat smoked tofu**
   or **firm tofu**, cut into 1 cm (½ inch) long strips
1 small handful **mint leaves**
1 small **carrot**, finely julienned
1 **cucumber**, peeled and julienned
1 handful **coriander (cilantro) leaves**

DIPPING SAUCE
4 tablespoons **hoisin sauce**
1 tablespoon **rice vinegar**
1 tablespoon **sugar**
1 tablespoon ground **roasted peanuts**
   (page 70)

Fill a large bowl with hot water. Taking one rice paper wrapper at a time, dip it into the water for about 15 seconds, or until soft, then lay out flat on a clean damp tea towel (dish towel). Lay a lettuce leaf over the wrapper, then put two pieces of tofu across the middle of each leaf. Top with two or three mint leaves, a little carrot, cucumber, coriander and vermicelli noodles. Fold the bottom of the wrapper up over the filling, then fold in the two sides. Roll up as tightly as possible with your hands. Keep each roll under a damp tea towel. Repeat with the rest of the wrappers and filling ingredients.

To make the dipping sauce, combine the ingredients (except the peanuts) and 2 tablespoons water in a small bowl and stir until the sugar dissolves. Transfer to a small serving dish and sprinkle with the peanuts. Allow two rice paper rolls for each person, and serve with the dipping sauce.

roasted duck and
coriander noodle salad
serves two to four

1 **Chinese roasted duck**

DRESSING
3 tablespoons **light soy sauce**
2 tablespoons **Chinese black vinegar**
1 tablespoon shaved **palm sugar (jaggery)**
or **soft brown sugar**
¼ teaspoon **sesame oil**
1 tablespoon **mirin** (optional)

SALAD
200 g (7 oz) **fresh coriander (cilantro) noodles** or other fresh
green noodles
8 **snow peas (mangetout)**, blanched and julienned
6 **baby corn**, blanched and cut into thin slices on the diagonal
1 handful **mint leaves**
1 handful **coriander (cilantro) leaves**
3 **red Asian shallots**, sliced

TO SERVE
1 tablespoon **roasted shredded coconut** (page 70)
1 tablespoon **roasted sesame seeds** (page 70)

Remove the skin and meat from the duck and thinly slice. Set aside. Combine all the dressing ingredients, stirring until the sugar dissolves.

To make the salad, put the coriander noodles in a bowl and cover with boiling water for 1 minute, or until softened, or follow the packet instructions. Refresh the noodles under cold water and drain well. Combine the noodles with the remaining salad ingredients, then pour over enough of the dressing to moisten the salad and toss to combine.

Arrange the noodle salad in individual serving bowls, top with the slices of duck and sprinkle with shredded coconut and sesame seeds. Serve any remaining dressing separately.

hokkien noodle salad with vegetables
serves four

SALAD
400 g (14 oz) **hokkien (egg) noodles**
2 **long red chillies**, seeded and julienned
5 **spring onions (scallions)**, julienned
40 g (1½ oz/1 cup) shredded **Chinese cabbage (wong bok)**
1 **carrot**, julienned
1 large handful **bean sprouts**, trimmed
1 handful **mixed fresh herbs**, such as Thai basil, mint, Vietnamese mint,
    coriander (cilantro) or sawtooth coriander (cilantro)

DRESSING
4 tablespoons **light soy sauce**
4 tablespoons **dark soy sauce**
2 tablespoons **Chinese black vinegar**
3 teaspoons **sesame oil**
pinch of **freshly ground black pepper**

Combine all the dressing ingredients in a bowl and mix well.

Pour hot water over the hokkien noodles to soften, then drain well. Refresh under cold water, then drain. Put the noodles and remaining salad ingredients in a bowl, season with salt and gently toss together. Pour in enough of the dressing to moisten the noodle salad and toss to combine. Serve any remaining salad dressing on the side.

spicy chinese-style noodles
serves four to six

2 tablespoons **vegetable oil**
1 **onion**, finely chopped
3 **garlic cloves**, crushed
300 g (10½ oz) **minced (ground) beef**
100 g (3½ oz/½ cup) finely chopped **preserved radish**
500 g (1 lb 2 oz) **dried thin wheat noodles**

DRESSING
4 tablespoons **dark soy sauce**
1½ tablespoons **Chinese black vinegar**
1½ tablespoons **chilli oil** (page 71)
1 teaspoon **sesame oil**
½ teaspoon **white pepper**
4 **spring onions (scallions)**, finely chopped

TO SERVE
1 handful **coriander (cilantro) leaves**, finely chopped

Heat the oil in a wok over high heat until smoking. Add the onion, garlic and beef and stir-fry for 3–4 minutes, or until the beef is cooked. Stir in the preserved radish. Set aside to cool slightly.

Combine the dressing ingredients in a bowl. Pour the dressing over the beef and radish, stir to combine and leave to cool to room temperature.

Cook the wheat noodles in boiling water for 1–2 minutes, or until soft, or follow the packet instructions. Drain and refresh under cold water, then drain again. To serve, place the noodles in individual serving bowls, top with the beef and radish mixture and sprinkle with coriander.

HINT _ Preserved radish is available from most Asian grocery stores.

grilled chicken
noodle salad
serves two to four

2 boneless, skinless chicken thighs
250 g (9 oz) hokkien (egg) noodles
1 tablespoon vegetable oil
1 long red chilli, seeded and julienned
1 small handful mint leaves
1 small handful coriander (cilantro) leaves

MARINADE
1 tablespoon finely grated fresh ginger
1 tablespoon caster (superfine) sugar
3 tablespoons oyster sauce
3 tablespoons shaoxing rice wine
1 tablespoon vegetable oil
2 garlic cloves, finely chopped

DRESSING
2 tablespoons light soy sauce
1/2 teaspoon sesame oil
1 tablespoon Chinese black vinegar
1 tablespoon caster (superfine) sugar
2 tablespoons lime juice

TO SERVE
1 tablespoon roasted sesame seeds (page 70)

Combine all the marinade ingredients in a large bowl. Add the chicken and toss to coat. Marinate in the refrigerator for at least 4 hours, or preferably overnight. Combine all the dressing ingredients, stirring until the sugar dissolves.

Pour hot water over the hokkien noodles to soften, then drain well. Refresh under cold water, then drain again.

Preheat a chargrill pan over medium heat. Add the oil and when it is hot, add the chicken and cook for 5–6 minutes on each side, or until cooked through. Remove from the pan and rest in a warm place for 5 minutes, then slice.

Combine the noodles, chilli, mint and coriander, add sufficient dressing to moisten, then gently mix. Pile the noodle salad onto a large serving plate or bowl, top with the sliced chicken and sprinkle with sesame seeds. Serve with any remaining dressing.

northern vietnamese turmeric fish fillet noodles serves four to six

400 g (14 oz) **firm white fish fillets**, such as ling or whiting, skinned and cut into thick slices
3 tablespoons **vegetable oil**
2 handfuls **dill**, roughly chopped
2 **spring onions (scallions)**, sliced

MARINADE
3 **garlic cloves**, peeled
4 cm (1½ inch) piece **fresh galangal**, sliced
pinch of **salt**
1 tablespoon **ground turmeric**
2 tablespoons **fish sauce**
pinch of **freshly ground black pepper**
1½ teaspoons **caster (superfine) sugar**
2 tablespoons **vegetable oil**
pinch of **chilli powder**

SALAD
200 g (7 oz) **rice vermicelli noodles**
1 handful **mint leaves**, roughly chopped
1 handful **Thai basil leaves**, roughly chopped
120 ml–160 ml (4 fl oz–5¼ fl oz) **nuoc cham** (page 71)

TO SERVE
4 tablespoons ground **roasted peanuts** (page 70)

To make the marinade, pound the garlic, galangal and salt into a paste using a mortar and pestle. Mix in the remaining marinade ingredients and stir until the sugar dissolves.

Put the fish slices in a bowl, pour over the marinade and mix to coat well. Cover and refrigerate for at least 4 hours, or preferably overnight.

To make the salad, put the vermicelli noodles in a bowl, cover with boiling water and soak for 5–7 minutes, or until softened. Drain well. Transfer to a large bowl, add the mint and Thai basil and gently mix in sufficient nuoc cham to moisten.

Heat the oil in a wok over high heat until smoking. Add the fish and stir-fry for 2–3 minutes. Add 3 tablespoons water and cook for a further 3 minutes, or until cooked. Toss in the dill and spring onion, then remove from the heat.

To serve, place the noodle salad in a large serving bowl, top with the fish and sprinkle with the peanuts. Serve warm or cold.

prawn and squid salad with glass noodles serves two to four

150 g (5½ oz) **bean thread vermicelli (glass) noodles**
3 cm (1¼ inch) piece **fresh ginger**, chopped
3 **garlic cloves**, chopped
2 small **red Asian shallots**, chopped
pinch of **salt**
1 tablespoon **vegetable oil**
200 g (7 oz) cleaned and prepared **squid**, cut into thin strips
500 g (1 lb 2 oz) **cooked prawns (shrimp)**, peeled and deveined, halved lengthways
1 handful **Thai basil leaves**
2 **spring onions (scallions)**, thinly sliced
1 handful **coriander (cilantro) leaves**

DRESSING
2 small **red chillies**, chopped
½ teaspoon **chilli flakes**
90 ml (3 fl oz) **lime juice**
2–3 tablespoons **fish sauce**
2 tablespoons **caster (superfine) sugar**

TO SERVE
2 tablespoons **fried shallots** (page 15)
2 tablespoons chopped **roasted peanuts** (page 70)
lime wedges

Soak the vermicelli noodles in boiling water for 5 minutes, then drain well. Cut the noodles into shorter lengths using scissors.

Using a mortar and pestle, pound the ginger, garlic, shallots and salt into a coarse paste. Heat the oil in a wok over high heat. Add the paste and stir-fry for 20–30 seconds until fragrant. Add the squid and stir-fry for 1 minute, or until the squid turns opaque. Remove from the heat and set aside.

Combine all the dressing ingredients, stirring until the sugar dissolves. Season to taste with extra fish sauce if necessary.

Combine the noodles, squid, prawns, Thai basil, spring onion and coriander. Add the dressing and toss to combine. To serve, transfer to a bowl and sprinkle with fried shallots and peanuts. Serve with lime wedges.

chicken soba noodles
serves four to six

1 tablespoon **salt**
200 g (7 oz) **soba (buckwheat) noodles**
125 ml (4 fl oz/1/2 cup) **chicken stock** (page 14)
4 tablespoons **shaoxing rice wine**
4 cm (11/2 inch) piece **fresh ginger**, sliced
1 **onion**, quartered
500 g (1 lb 2 oz) **boneless, skinless chicken breast**

DRESSING
1 tablespoon **mirin**
2 tablespoons **Chinese black vinegar**
2 tablespoons **light soy sauce**
2 tablespoons **vegetable oil**
2 teaspoons **sesame oil**
1 tablespoon **lime juice**
2 **spring onions (scallions)**, thinly sliced

TO SERVE
1 tablespoon **roasted sesame seeds** (page 70)

Put 3 litres (105 fl oz/12 cups) water into a large saucepan, add the salt and bring to the boil. Add the soba noodles and cook for 4–5 minutes, uncovered, or follow the packet instructions. Drain, refresh under cold water, then drain well again. Cover and refrigerate.

Put the stock, wine, ginger and onion in a large saucepan. Bring to the boil, then add the chicken and simmer for 6 minutes. Turn off the heat and cover with a lid, allowing the chicken to cool in the stock—it will continue to cook during this time. Remove the chicken from the stock. Use your hands or a fork to shred the meat. Discard the stock.

Combine all the dressing ingredients and mix well. Combine the chicken and noodles in a bowl, add sufficient dressing to moisten and gently mix. To serve, pile the noodle mixture into a large bowl and sprinkle with sesame seeds. Serve with any remaining dressing.

chinese noodles with sesame dressing serves two to four

300 g (10½ oz) **dried thin wheat noodles**
2 handfuls **bean sprouts**, trimmed

DRESSING
2 tablespoons **light soy sauce**
2 tablespoons **kecap manis**
1 tablespoon **sesame oil**
2 tablespoons **Chinese black vinegar**
2 teaspoons **chilli oil** (page 71)
2 **bird's eye chillies**, seeded and thinly sliced
1 tablespoon julienned **fresh ginger**
2 tablespoons finely chopped **coriander**
  (cilantro) roots, stems and leaves

TO SERVE
2 **spring onions (scallions)**, thinly sliced
1 tablespoon **roasted sesame seeds** (page 70)

Cook the wheat noodles in boiling water for 1–2 minutes, or until softened, or follow the packet instructions. Drain, refresh under cold water, then drain well again. Blanch the bean sprouts in hot water for 30 seconds, then drain.

Combine all the dressing ingredients in a bowl and stir well.

Combine the noodles and bean sprouts in a bowl. Add sufficient dressing to moisten the noodles and gently mix. Place the noodles into a serving bowl and sprinkle with spring onion and sesame seeds. Serve with any remaining dressing.

lemon grass beef with rice vermicelli salad serves four to six

400 g (14 oz) **beef rump** or **sirloin steak**, thinly sliced

3 tablespoons **vegetable oil**

MARINADE

2 **lemon grass stems**, white part only, finely chopped

3 **garlic cloves**, peeled

1 teaspoon **salt**

1 **onion**, halved and thinly sliced

1/2 teaspoon **freshly ground black pepper**

1 tablespoon **fish sauce**

1/2 teaspoon **caster (superfine) sugar**

SALAD

150 g (5 1/2 oz) **rice vermicelli noodles**

2 large handfuls **bean sprouts**, trimmed

1 small handful **mint leaves**, sliced

1 small handful **coriander (cilantro) leaves**

1 small **carrot**, julienned

1 **Lebanese (short) cucumber**, seeded and julienned

2 **iceberg lettuce leaves**, roughly chopped

1 **lemon grass stem**, soft inner part only, finely chopped

120 ml–160 ml (4 fl oz–5 1/4 fl oz) **nuoc cham** (page 71)

TO SERVE

2 tablespoons chopped **roasted peanuts** (page 70)

2 tablespoons **fried shallots** (page 15)

lime wedges

To make the marinade, pound the lemon grass, garlic and salt into a paste using a mortar and pestle. Stir in the remaining marinade ingredients. Put the sliced beef in a bowl, add the marinade and mix to coat well. Marinate in the refrigerator for 4 hours, or preferably overnight.

To make the salad, place the vermicelli noodles in a bowl, cover with boiling water and leave to soak for 5–7 minutes, or until softened. Drain well. Transfer the noodles to a large bowl, add the bean sprouts, mint, coriander, carrot, cucumber and lettuce and gently mix well. Combine the lemon grass and nuoc cham and add to the salad. Toss well to coat.

Heat the oil in a wok over high heat until smoking. Working in batches, add the beef to the wok and stir-fry for 3–4 minutes, or until cooked. Remove from the heat.

Put the salad into a serving bowl and top with the beef. Sprinkle with the roasted peanuts and fried shallots and serve with lime wedges for squeezing over the salad.

smoked salmon with somen noodles
serves four

200 g (7 oz) **somen noodles**
250 g (9 oz) **smoked salmon**
20 g (3/4 oz/1 small bunch) **chives**, finely snipped
2–3 **red Asian shallots**, thinly sliced
2 small **ripe avocados**, cubed

DRESSING
4 tablespoons **vegetable oil**
2½ tablespoons **Chinese black vinegar**
1 tablespoon **lime juice**
1 tablespoon **mirin**
2 teaspoons **wasabi**

TO SERVE
2 teaspoons **roasted sesame seeds** (page 70)
2 teaspoons **roasted black sesame seeds** (page 70)

Cook the somen noodles in a large saucepan of boiling water for 2 minutes, or until just tender. Drain, rinse under cold water, then drain well again. Tear the smoked salmon into bite-sized pieces.

Combine all the dressing ingredients and stir well. In a separate bowl, gently combine the salmon, chives, shallots and avocado.

To serve, divide the noodles among individual plates. Spoon over some dressing, then scatter over the salmon and avocado mixture. Sprinkle with the combined toasted sesame seeds. Serve with any remaining dressing.

prawn, pork and rice noodle salad with chilli, lime and coconut dressing
serves four to six

1 teaspoon **salt**
250 g (9 oz) **pork neck fillet**
200 g (7 oz) **dried rice noodles** (preferably the round *bun* type)
1 handful **Thai basil leaves**, sliced
1 **Lebanese (short) cucumber**, seeded and julienned
1 handful **bean sprouts**, trimmed
250 g (9 oz) **cooked prawns (shrimp)**, peeled and deveined, halved lengthways

DRESSING
120 ml (4 fl oz) **nuoc cham** (page 71)
2 tablespoons **fish sauce**
160 ml (5¼ fl oz) **coconut cream**

TO SERVE
2 tablespoons **fried shallots** (page 15)
lime wedges

Put 1.5 litres (52 fl oz/6 cups) water in a large saucepan, add the salt and bring to the boil. Carefully add the pork fillet and return to the boil, then reduce the heat and simmer for 6 minutes. Cover the pan, turn off the heat and leave the pork to cool in the water. Once cooled, remove the pork from the water and thinly slice.

Place the rice noodles in a bowl, cover with boiling water and soak for 5–7 minutes, or until softened, or follow the packet instructions. Drain, refresh under cold water, then drain well.

Combine all the dressing ingredients and mix well.

Combine the noodles with the Thai basil, cucumber and bean sprouts. Add sufficient dressing to moisten the salad and mix well. Season to taste. Transfer to a serving bowl, and top with the sliced pork and prawns. Garnish with fried shallots and serve with lime wedges and any remaining dressing.

grilled beef hokkien noodle
salad serves four

3 x 150 g (5½ oz) **beef rump** or **sirloin steaks**, trimmed
1 tablespoon **peanut oil**
400 g (14 oz) **hokkien (egg) noodles**

DRESSING
185 ml (6 fl oz/¾ cup) **sweet chilli sauce** (page 108)
2 tablespoons **fish sauce**
3 tablespoons **lime juice**
1 tablespoon **white vinegar**
pinch of **chilli flakes**

SALAD
2 **long red chillies**, seeded and julienned
1 handful **Thai basil leaves**
1 handful **mint leaves**
1 handful **coriander (cilantro) leaves**
2 **spring onions (scallions)**, thinly sliced

TO SERVE
2 tablespoons chopped **roasted peanuts** (page 70)
2 tablespoons **fried shallots** (page 15)

Heat a chargrill pan over medium–high heat. Brush the beef with the oil, then cook for about 3 minutes on each side, or until cooked to medium. Rest in a warm place for 5 minutes, then slice thinly.

Pour hot water over the hokkien noodles to soften them, then drain well. Transfer to a large bowl and loosen the noodles with your fingers.

Combine the dressing ingredients and mix well. Combine the salad ingredients, add the beef, then toss into the noodles. Add sufficient dressing to moisten and mix gently.

To serve, divide the beef noodle salad among serving plates and sprinkle with the peanuts and fried shallots. Serve with any remaining dressing.

central vietnam noodles
serves four

3 **garlic cloves**, peeled
1 **lemon grass stem**, white part only, finely chopped
pinch of **salt**
pinch of **freshly ground black pepper**
1/2 teaspoon **ground star anise**
1/2 teaspoon **ground cinnamon**
2 tablespoons **caster (superfine) sugar**
250 g (9 oz) **pork neck fillet**, sliced
2 tablespoons **fish sauce**
125 ml (4 fl oz/1/2 cup) **soy sauce**
3 tablespoons **vegetable oil**

SALAD
250 g (9 oz) **dried rice noodles** (preferably the round *bun* type)
1 handful **bean sprouts**, trimmed
1 handful **Thai basil leaves**, sliced
1 handful **mint leaves**, sliced
1 handful **coriander (cilantro) leaves**

TO SERVE
2 tablespoons **fried shallots** (page 15)
3 tablespoons chopped **roasted peanuts** (page 70)
chilli and rice vinegar (page 71)

Using a mortar and pestle, pound the garlic, lemon grass and salt into a thick paste. Work in the pepper, star anise, cinnamon and sugar. Put the slices of pork in a bowl, add the paste and mix well to coat. Cover and marinate in the refrigerator for at least 4 hours, or preferably overnight.

Combine the fish sauce and soy sauce with 150 ml (5 fl oz) water. Heat the oil in a wok over high heat until smoking. Add the pork and stir-fry for 3–4 minutes. Add the fish sauce mixture and simmer for a further 6 minutes, or until cooked. Leave the pork to cool in the sauce.

To make the salad, place the rice noodles in a bowl, cover with boiling water and soak for 5–7 minutes, or until softened, or follow the packet instructions. Drain, refresh under cold water, then drain well again. Combine the noodles with the remaining salad ingredients, adding some of the sauce to moisten, and gently mix.

To serve, divide the salad between individual serving bowls and top with the pork and remaining sauce. Sprinkle with fried shallots and peanuts and serve the chilli and vinegar sauce on the side.

pork salad with glass noodles, mint and ginger serves four to six

2 tablespoons **oil**
2 **garlic cloves**, crushed
500 g (1 lb 2 oz) **minced (ground) pork**

SALAD
150 g (5½ oz) **bean thread vermicelli (glass) noodles**
1 handful **mint leaves**, torn in half if large
1 handful **coriander (cilantro) leaves**
1 large **spring onion (scallion)**, thinly sliced
1 small **red Asian shallot**, thinly sliced
2 tablespoons finely julienned **fresh ginger**
4 tablespoons **roasted peanuts**, chopped (page 70)
2 **makrut (kaffir lime) leaves**, finely shredded
1 **long red chilli**, seeded and julienned

DRESSING
2 small **bird's eye chillies**, sliced
1/2 teaspoon **chilli flakes**
3 tablespoons **fish sauce**
1½ teaspoons **caster (superfine) sugar**
4 tablespoons **lime juice**

TO SERVE
large wedges of **white cabbage**

Heat the oil in a wok over high heat until smoking. Add the garlic and pork and stir-fry for 3–4 minutes. Add 3 tablespoons water and simmer for about 2 minutes, or until the pork is cooked. Remove from the heat and leave to cool to room temperature.

To make the salad, soak the vermicelli noodles in boiling water for 5 minutes, then drain well. Cut the noodles into shorter lengths using scissors.

Combine all the dressing ingredients and stir until the sugar dissolves. Combine the pork and noodles with the remaining salad ingredients, add sufficient dressing to moisten and gently mix. To serve, transfer the pork salad to a large serving bowl and serve accompanied with wedges of cabbage.

03**STIR-FRY**RECIPES

When it comes to stir-frying, the Chinese use the phrase *wok hei*, or 'the breath of the wok', which refers to the wonderful aroma and heat-seared flavour of food cooked to perfection in a hot wok. This is what I love most about stir-frying—the way the heat seals in the colour, flavour and goodness of the food, and the deliciously smoky flavours you get from the wok. Noodles are great in stir-fries, either as the main ingredient or as the supporting role, along with fresh vegetables, seafood or meat. They usually need only a bit of soaking to soften them a little, then they can be tossed into the wok along with the other ingredients. I often use hokkien noodles for stir-frying because of their firm texture and thickness, which enables them to pick up more sauce. Dried egg noodles and rice vermicelli are good too, but I really love rice noodles for their soft, velvety texture and the way they soak up the flavours of the sauce. To achieve your own *wok hei* you need to prepare all your ingredients and mix up your sauces before you start. Then, get the wok really hot and work quickly—once you start, you've got to keep going!

BASICS

sweet chilli sauce

3 **garlic cloves**, peeled
3 **long red chillies**
500 ml (17 fl oz/2 cups) **rice vinegar**
330 g (11½ oz/1½ cups) **sugar**
1 teaspoon **salt**

Use a mortar and pestle to pound the garlic and chillies to form a paste. Alternatively, chop them into a paste using a small food processor.

Combine all the ingredients and 500 ml (17 fl oz/ 2 cups) water in a saucepan and bring to the boil. Reduce the heat, then simmer until reduced by half, or until the mixture thickens to a slightly syrupy consistency. Remove and allow to cool. Store in the refrigerator for up to 1 month or freeze in small portions.

Makes 750 ml (26 fl oz/3 cups)

spicy satay paste

4 **spring onions (scallions)**, white part only, roughly chopped
2 tablespoons **vegetable oil**
6 **garlic cloves**, finely chopped
2 tablespoons finely chopped **lemon grass**
1 tablespoon **chilli flakes**
1 tablespoon **soy sauce**
1½ tablespoons **sugar**
1 teaspoon **salt**

Put the chopped spring onion in a small food processor and blend to a paste.

Heat the oil in a wok over high heat. Fry the spring onion, garlic and lemon grass until fragrant. Remove from the heat and add the remaining ingredients. Stir well, then leave to cool. This paste will keep for up to 1 week in an airtight jar in the refrigerator, covered with a thin layer of oil.

Makes about 175 g (6 oz)

vegetable stock

2 tablespoons **vegetable oil**
2 slices **fresh ginger**
2 **garlic cloves**, crushed
2 **spring onions (scallions)**, cut into 3 cm
(1¼ inch) lengths
1 **onion**, roughly chopped
1 **carrot**, roughly chopped
1 **daikon**, roughly chopped
2 **celery stalks**, roughly chopped

Heat the oil in a large saucepan, add the ginger, garlic and vegetables and stir-fry until fragrant. Add 3 litres (105 fl oz/12 cups) water and bring to the boil. Reduce the heat and simmer for 30 minutes. Leave to cool, then strain. Store the stock in the refrigerator for up to 3 days or freeze in small portions for up to 6 months.

Makes about 2.75 litres (96 fl oz/11 cups)

chilli jam

60 g (2¼ oz/½ cup) **dried shrimp**
40 **dried long red chillies**
vegetable oil, for deep-frying
12 **red Asian shallots**, sliced lengthways
20 **garlic cloves**, sliced lengthways
4 tablespoons **fish sauce**
85 g (3 oz) shaved **palm sugar (jaggery)**
2 tablespoons **tamarind water** (page 14)

Soak the dried shrimp in hot water for 10–15 minutes, or until softened. Drain, then dry thoroughly. Discard the seeds and stems from the dried chillies, then soak in hot water for 10 minutes. Drain, pat dry and roughly chop.

Fill a wok or deep-fat fryer one-third full of oil and heat to 180°C (350°F), or until a cube of bread dropped into the oil browns in 15 seconds. Cooking each ingredient separately, deep-fry the shallots, garlic, chopped chillies and dried shrimp until golden, being very careful not to burn any of the ingredients. Drain on paper towels. Allow the oil to cool.

Using a mortar and pestle, pound the deep-fried shallots, garlic, chillies and shrimp into a paste with 4–5 tablespoons of the cooled oil from the wok. Alternatively, chop the ingredients into a paste using a small food processor.

In a hot wok, bring the paste to the boil and season with the fish sauce, palm sugar and tamarind water. Reduce the heat and simmer, stirring regularly, until quite thick. Remove and allow to cool. Store in an airtight jar for up to 3 weeks in the refrigerator.

Makes about 300 g (10½ oz/1 cup)

malaysian-style stir-fried egg noodles with chinese vegetables
serves two to four

200 g (7 oz) **hokkien (egg) noodles**
3 tablespoons **vegetable oil**
100 g (3½ oz) **firm tofu**, sliced
150 g (5½ oz) **Chinese broccoli (gai larn)**,
   cut into 3 cm (1¼ inch) lengths
100 g (3½ oz) **choy sum**, cut into 5 cm (2 inch)
   lengths
150 g (5½ oz) **baby corn**, cut into thirds on
   the diagonal
3 tablespoons **vegetable stock** (page 109)
   or **water**
1 tablespoon **oyster sauce**
1 tablespoon **dark soy sauce**
1 handful **bean sprouts**, trimmed

PASTE
2 **dried long red chillies**
1 **garlic clove**, peeled
2 **red Asian shallots**, peeled
pinch of **salt**

TO SERVE
1 handful **coriander (cilantro) leaves**
lime wedges

To make the paste, discard the seeds and stems from the dried chillies, then soak in hot water for 10 minutes. Drain, then roughly chop. Using a mortar and pestle, pound the chillies, garlic, shallots and salt into a paste.

Rinse the hokkien noodles under warm water to separate them, then drain.

Heat the oil in a hot wok and fry the paste until fragrant. Add the tofu and stir-fry for 1 minute. Add the noodles, Chinese broccoli, choy sum and baby corn and stir-fry for 2 minutes. Add the stock, oyster sauce, soy sauce and bean sprouts and stir-fry for another 1 minute.

Pile the noodles into serving bowls. Garnish with coriander and serve with lime wedges.

HINT _ Omit the oyster sauce for a vegetarian meal.

barbecued duck
hokkien noodles
serves two to four

300 g (10 1/2 oz) **hokkien (egg) noodles**
1/2 **Chinese barbecued duck**
3 tablespoons **vegetable oil**
2 **garlic cloves**, crushed
150 g (5 1/2 oz) **baby bok choy (pak choy)**, cut into
quarters lengthways
1 1/2 tablespoons **oyster sauce**
1 1/2 tablespoons **light soy sauce**
pinch of **salt**
pinch of **white pepper**

TO SERVE
1 small handful **bean sprouts**, trimmed
1 **spring onion (scallion)**, thinly sliced on the diagonal

Rinse the hokkien noodles under warm water to separate them, then drain. Remove the skin and meat from the duck and cut into strips.

Heat the oil in a hot wok. Add the garlic and stir-fry for 20–30 seconds until fragrant. Add the noodles and stir-fry for 1 minute, or until the noodles are slightly soft. Add the duck and bok choy and stir-fry for a further 1–2 minutes. Add the oyster sauce, soy sauce, salt, white pepper and 3 tablespoons water and stir-fry for about 1 minute, or until the noodles have absorbed most of the liquid.

To serve, pile the noodles into a bowl, top with bean sprouts and sprinkle with spring onion.

beef chow mein
serves two to four

150 g (5½ oz) **beef rump** or **tenderloin**, thinly sliced
150 g (5½ oz) **dried thick egg noodles**
2 tablespoons **vegetable oil**
1 **onion**, thinly sliced
1 small **red capsicum (pepper)**, julienned
20 g (¾ oz/ ½ cup) shredded **Chinese cabbage (wong bok)**
1 handful **bean sprouts**, trimmed

SAUCE
1 tablespoon **shaoxing rice wine**
1 tablespoon **light soy sauce**
1 tablespoon **dark soy sauce**
pinch of **sugar**
pinch of **salt**

MARINADE
1 **garlic clove**, finely chopped
½ teaspoon **sesame oil**
1 teaspoon **light soy sauce**
pinch of **freshly ground black pepper**

TO SERVE
2 **spring onions (scallions)**, thinly sliced on the diagonal

Combine the marinade ingredients in a bowl and mix well. Add the sliced beef and toss to coat. Marinate in the refrigerator for 30 minutes.

Soak the noodles in warm water for 20 minutes, then drain. Combine all the sauce ingredients and set aside.

Heat the oil in a wok over high heat. Add the beef and stir-fry for 2 minutes, then add the onion, capsicum and Chinese cabbage and stir-fry for 2–3 minutes, or until the vegetables are just cooked. Add the noodles and bean sprouts, pour in the sauce and stir-fry for a further 1–2 minutes.

To serve, pile the noodles and beef onto a serving plate and sprinkle with spring onion.

crispy noodles with vegetables
serves two to four

vegetable oil, for deep-frying
200 g (7 oz) **fresh thin egg noodles**
1 **garlic clove**, crushed
150 g (5½ oz/1 bunch) **asparagus**, sliced into 2 cm (¾ inch) lengths
   on the diagonal
2 **baby bok choy (pak choy)**, cut into quarters lengthways
150 g (5½ oz) **snow peas (mangetout)**, halved on the diagonal
4 large **oyster mushrooms**, roughly torn
150 g (5½ oz) **baby corn**, sliced in half on the diagonal
125 ml (4 fl oz/½ cup) **vegetable stock** or **water**
3 tablespoons **shaoxing rice wine**
1 tablespoon **light soy sauce**
1 tablespoon **dark soy sauce**
2 teaspoons **sugar**
½ teaspoon **sesame oil**
1 teaspoon **salt**
1 tablespoon **cornflour (cornstarch)**

TO SERVE
coriander (cilantro) leaves (optional)
pinch of **white pepper**

Fill a wok or deep-fat fryer one-third full of oil and heat to 180°C (350°F), or until a cube of bread dropped into the oil browns in 15 seconds. Carefully add the egg noodles and deep-fry for 20–30 seconds, or until puffed and golden. Drain on paper towels and keep warm. Clean out the wok, reserving 1 tablespoon of the oil.

Heat the reserved oil in a hot wok. Add the garlic and stir-fry for 20–30 seconds until fragrant. Add all the vegetables and stir-fry for 2–3 minutes, or until the vegetables just start to wilt but are still crisp. Transfer to a warm dish.

Clean out the wok and pour in the stock, wine, light soy sauce, dark soy sauce, sugar, sesame oil and salt. Bring to the boil. Meanwhile, combine the cornflour with 1 tablespoon water. Return the vegetables to the wok, then pour in the cornflour mixture, stirring constantly until the sauce thickens. To serve, put the crispy noodles on a plate and top with the vegetables. Garnish with coriander (if using) and sprinkle with white pepper.

pad thai
serves one to two

150 g (5½ oz) **dried rice stick noodles**
1 tablespoon **dried shrimp**
vegetable oil, for deep-frying
50 g (1¾ oz) **firm tofu**, cut into thin, 2 cm (¾ inch) long strips
¼ **onion**, thinly sliced
2 **eggs**, lightly beaten
1 large handful **bean sprouts**, trimmed
25 g (1 oz/¼ bunch) **garlic chives**, cut into 2 cm (¾ inch) lengths

SAUCE
1½ tablespoons **fish sauce**
1 tablespoon shaved **palm sugar (jaggery)**
1 tablespoon **tamarind water** (page 14)
1 tablespoon **oyster sauce**

TO SERVE
1 tablespoon chopped **roasted peanuts** (page 70)
lime wedges

Soak the noodles in cold water for 30 minutes, or until softened, then drain. Meanwhile, soak the dried shrimp in hot water for 10–15 minutes, or until softened. Drain, then chop.

Combine the sauce ingredients in a small saucepan and simmer over low heat, stirring until the sugar dissolves.

Fill a wok or deep-fat fryer one-third full of oil and heat to 180°C (350°F), or until a cube of bread dropped into the oil browns in 15 seconds. Deep-fry the tofu for 1 minute, or until lightly golden. Drain on paper towels. Clean out the wok, reserving 1 tablespoon of the oil.

Heat the reserved oil in a hot wok. Add the onion and stir-fry for about 1 minute, or until fragrant. Stir in the beaten egg, then add the tofu, dried shrimp and noodles and stir-fry for 1 minute. Pour in the sauce and simmer for 30 seconds. Toss in the bean sprouts and garlic chives and stir-fry for 30 seconds.

To serve, pile the noodles onto a plate and sprinkle with roasted peanuts. Serve with lime wedges.

egg noodles with beef and vegetables serves two

2 **dried shiitake mushrooms**
150 g (5½ oz) **dried thick egg noodles**
150 g (5½ oz) **beef rump steak**, thinly sliced
2 tablespoons **vegetable oil**
1 **garlic clove**, finely chopped
1 teaspoon finely grated **fresh ginger**
50 g (1¾ oz/1 cup) thinly sliced **Chinese cabbage (wong bok)**
½ **carrot**, julienned
1 handful **bean sprouts**, trimmed
25 g (1 oz/¼ bunch) **garlic chives**, cut into 3 cm (1¼ inch) lengths

MARINADE
1 tablespoon **shaoxing rice wine**
pinch of **salt**
pinch of **freshly ground black pepper**

SAUCE
2 tablespoons **chicken stock** (page 14) or **water**
1 tablespoon **light soy sauce**
1½ tablespoons **oyster sauce**
½ teaspoon **sesame oil**
pinch of **freshly ground black pepper**

TO SERVE
1 small handful **coriander (cilantro) leaves**

Soak the mushrooms in hot water until softened. Drain, discard the stems and thinly slice the caps. Soak the noodles in warm water for 20 minutes, then drain well.

Combine the marinade ingredients in a bowl. Add the sliced beef and stir to coat. Combine all the sauce ingredients and set aside.

Heat the oil in a wok over high heat. Add the beef to the wok and stir-fry for 1 minute. Add the garlic and ginger and stir-fry for 20–30 seconds until fragrant.

Toss in the mushrooms, cabbage and carrot and cook until the cabbage starts to wilt, then add the noodles and bean sprouts and stir-fry for 1 minute. Pour in the sauce and cook for 2 minutes, or until the noodles have absorbed most of the liquid. Stir in the garlic chives.

To serve, pile the noodles onto a serving plate and garnish with coriander.

fried rice noodles with vegetables
serves two to four

3 tablespoons **vegetable oil**
250 g (9 oz) **fresh rice sheet noodles**, cut into 1 cm (1/2 inch) wide strips
1 tablespoon **oyster sauce**
2 tablespoons **dark soy sauce**
1 **garlic clove**, crushed
1 teaspoon grated **fresh ginger**
150 g (5½ oz) **Chinese broccoli (gai larn)**, cut into 3 cm (1¼ inch) lengths
125 g (4½ oz) **snow peas (mangetout)**, halved on the diagonal
150 (5½ oz) **baby corn**, halved on the diagonal
1 tablespoon **cornflour (cornstarch)**
1 tablespoon **light soy sauce**
pinch of **salt**

TO SERVE
1 small handful **coriander (cilantro) leaves**
pinch of **white pepper**
soy sauce

Heat 2 tablespoons of the oil in a hot wok. Add the noodles and stir-fry for about 1 minute. Add the oyster sauce and 1 tablespoon of the dark soy sauce and stir-fry for a further 30 seconds. Remove the noodles from the wok and keep warm.

Heat the remaining tablespoon of oil in the hot wok. Add the garlic and ginger and stir-fry for 20–30 seconds until fragrant. Add the Chinese broccoli, snow peas, baby corn and 125 ml (4 fl oz/½ cup) water. Bring the liquid to the boil.

Meanwhile, mix the cornflour with 1 tablespoon water. When the liquid in the wok is boiling, add the light soy sauce, remaining tablespoon of dark soy sauce and the salt. Slowly pour in the cornflour mixture, stirring constantly until the sauce thickens.

To serve, put the warm noodles in a shallow bowl. Spoon the vegetables over the top and sprinkle with coriander and white pepper. Serve accompanied with soy sauce.

HINT _ Omit the oyster sauce for a vegetarian meal.

combo egg noodles
serves two to four

180 g (6 oz) **dried thin egg noodles**
2 tablespoons **vegetable oil**
80 g (2¾ oz) **boneless, skinless chicken breast**, thinly sliced
1 **garlic clove**, finely chopped
8 **raw prawns (shrimp)**, peeled and deveined, tails left intact
100 g (3½ oz) **baby bok choy (pak choy)**, cut into quarters lengthways
80 g (2¾ oz) **Chinese barbecued pork (char siu)**, thinly sliced
1 small **carrot**, julienned
3 **spring onions (scallions)**, cut into 3 cm (1¼ inch) lengths
1 handful **bean sprouts**, trimmed
1 small handful **coriander (cilantro) leaves**

SAUCE
2 ½ tablespoons **oyster sauce**
pinch of **freshly ground black pepper**

Soak the noodles in warm water for 20 minutes, then drain well. Combine the sauce ingredients with 2 tablespoons water and set aside.

Heat the oil in a wok until smoking. Add the chicken and garlic and stir-fry for 1 minute. Add the prawns and stir-fry for a further 2–3 minutes, or until the prawns and chicken are nearly cooked. Add the bok choy, pork, carrot, spring onion and 3 tablespoons water. Cook for 2 minutes, or until the bok choy is cooked. Add the noodles, bean sprouts and sauce. Season with salt and cook for another 2 minutes. Scatter over the coriander and serve.

chicken egg noodles with teriyaki
sauce   serves two to four

250 g (9 oz) **boneless, skinless chicken breast**,
  thinly sliced
2 tablespoons **teriyaki sauce**
250 g (9 oz) **dried thin egg noodles**
70 g (2½ oz) **white cabbage**, cut into 3 cm
  (1¼ inch) strips
1 small **carrot**, juliénned
3 tablespoons **vegetable oil**
½ **onion**, thinly sliced
2 **garlic cloves**, finely chopped
1 handful **bean sprouts**, trimmed
2 **spring onions (scallions)**, cut into 3 cm
  (1¼ inch) lengths
1 handful **coriander (cilantro) leaves**

SAUCE
4 tablespoons **teriyaki sauce**
1 tablespoon **light soy sauce**
pinch of **freshly ground black pepper**

Marinate the sliced chicken in the teriyaki sauce and set aside in the refrigerator.

Soak the egg noodles in warm water for 20 minutes, then drain well. Blanch the cabbage and carrot in boiling water for 1 minute, then refresh under cold water. Drain well.

Combine the sauce ingredients with 3 tablespoons water and set aside.

Heat the oil in a wok over high heat until smoking. Add the onion, garlic and chicken and stir-fry for 3–4 minutes, or until the chicken is just cooked. Pour in the sauce, then add the noodles, cabbage, carrot and bean sprouts and cook until the sauce has reduced. Add the spring onion and stir through. Scatter over the coriander and serve.

scallops with egg noodles and chinese broccoli

serves two to four

200 g (7 oz) **dried thick egg noodles**
300 g (10½ oz/1 bunch) **Chinese broccoli
  (gai larn)**, cut into 3 cm (1¼ inch) lengths,
  thick stems halved lengthways
3 tablespoons **vegetable oil**
12 **scallops**, roe removed
2 **garlic cloves**, finely chopped

SAUCE
1 teaspoon **sesame oil**
1 tablespoon **light soy sauce**
2 tablespoons **oyster sauce**
½ teaspoon **sugar**
pinch of **freshly ground black pepper**

TO SERVE
1 **long red chilli**, seeded and sliced
2 **spring onions (scallions)**, thinly sliced on the diagonal
1 small handful **coriander (cilantro) leaves**

Soak the noodles in warm water for 20 minutes, or until softened, then drain. Blanch the Chinese broccoli in boiling water for 1 minute. Refresh under cold water, then drain well.

Heat 1 tablespoon of the oil in a wok over high heat until smoking. Sear the scallops for 1 minute on each side. Do this in batches so as not to overcrowd the wok. Drain the scallops on paper towels.

Combine the sauce ingredients with 4 tablespoons water, stirring until the sugar dissolves.

Heat the remaining 2 tablespoons of oil in the wok over high heat until smoking. Stir-fry the garlic until fragrant, then add the noodles and Chinese broccoli and cook for 1 minute. Add the sauce and scallops and cook until most of the liquid has been absorbed. Transfer the noodles to a large serving plate or individual bowls and sprinkle with chilli, spring onion and coriander.

chicken rice noodles with sweet chilli sauce serves two to four

150 g (5½ oz) **dried thin rice noodles** or **rice stick noodles**
2 tablespoons **oil**
250 g (9 oz) **boneless, skinless chicken breast**, thinly sliced
1 **onion**, thinly sliced
1 **garlic clove**, finely chopped
100 g (3½ oz) **broccoli**, cut into bite-sized pieces
80 g (2¾ oz) **snow peas (mangetout)**, julienned
1 handful **bean sprouts**, trimmed

SAUCE
4 tablespoons **sweet chilli sauce** (page 108)
2–3 tablespoons **oyster sauce**

TO SERVE
2 **spring onions (scallions)**, thinly sliced
1 small handful **coriander (cilantro) leaves**

Soak the rice noodles in cold water for 30 minutes, or until softened, then drain well. Combine the sauce ingredients with 2 tablespoons water and set aside.

Heat the oil in a wok over high heat until smoking. Add the chicken, onion and garlic and stir-fry for 2–3 minutes, or until the chicken is almost cooked. Add the broccoli, snow peas and 2 tablespoons water and cook for 2 minutes. Toss in the noodles and bean sprouts, then pour in the sauce and stir-fry for about 2 minutes, or until the noodles have absorbed most of the sauce.

To serve, put the noodles in individual bowls or on a serving plate and sprinkle with spring onion and coriander.

spicy beef hokkien noodles
serves two to four

150 g (5½ oz) **beef rump** or **tenderloin**, thinly sliced
1 **garlic clove**, finely chopped
1 small **onion**, thinly sliced
2 tablespoons **vegetable oil**
200 g (7 oz) **hokkien (egg) noodles**
75 g (2½ oz/1 cup) thinly sliced **cabbage**
1 small **carrot**, julienned
2 **spring onions (scallions)**, thinly sliced
40 g (1½ oz) **green beans**, thinly sliced on the diagonal
1 **tomato**, cut into wedges

SAUCE
2 teaspoons **spicy satay paste** (page 108)
1½ tablespoons **oyster sauce**

TO SERVE
1 small handful **coriander (cilantro) leaves**
1 **long red chilli**, seeded and sliced

Combine the sliced beef with the garlic, onion and 1 tablespoon of the oil. Marinate in the refrigerator for 15–20 minutes.

Rinse the hokkien noodles under warm water to separate them, then drain well. Combine the sauce ingredients with 4 tablespoons water and set aside.

Heat the remaining 1 tablespoon of oil in a wok over high heat until smoking. Stir-fry the beef and its marinade for 1–2 minutes, or until the beef is half cooked. Add the cabbage, carrot, spring onion, beans and tomato and stir-fry for 3–4 minutes. Pour in the sauce, then toss in the noodles and stir-fry until the noodles have absorbed most of the sauce.

To serve, pile the noodles into a serving bowl and sprinkle with coriander and chilli.

rice vermicelli pancake with prawns and vegetables serves two to four

150 g (5½ oz) **rice vermicelli noodles**
100 ml (3½ fl oz) **vegetable oil**
1 **garlic clove**, finely chopped
10 **raw king prawns (shrimp)**, peeled and
   deveined
½ teaspoon finely grated **fresh ginger**
4 **baby corn**, halved lengthways
½ **carrot**, cut into thin slices on the diagonal
40 g (1½ oz) **broccoli**, cut into bite-sized
   pieces
2 **spring onions (scallions)**, cut into 3 cm
   (1¼ inch) lengths
1 small handful **bean sprouts**, trimmed

SAUCE
100 ml (3½ fl oz) **chicken stock** (page 14)
2 tablespoons **oyster sauce**
1 teaspoon **light soy sauce**
pinch of **sugar**
pinch of **freshly ground black pepper**
½ teaspoon **cornflour (cornstarch)**

Soak the vermicelli noodles in cold water for 30 minutes, or until softened. Drain well. Combine the sauce ingredients, mix well and set aside.

Heat 3 tablespoons of the oil in a non-stick frying pan over medium–high heat. Add the noodles and shape them into a pancake about 25 cm (10 inches) in diameter. Cook for about 6 minutes, or until the noodle pancake is crisp and golden underneath. Turn the pancake over and cook the other side for 3–4 minutes, or until golden. Remove from the heat and set aside.

Heat the remaining oil in a wok, add the garlic and stir-fry for 20–30 seconds until fragrant. Add the prawns and ginger and stir-fry for 1–2 minutes, or until the prawns turn pink. Add the baby corn, carrot, broccoli and spring onion and stir-fry for 2 minutes. Stir in the bean sprouts, then pour in the sauce and cook until the sauce starts to thicken.

To serve, cut the vermicelli pancake into eight pieces. Place onto a serving plate and top with the prawns and vegetables.

hokkien noodles with seafood
and chilli jam serves two

1 **squid tube**
200 g (7 oz) **hokkien (egg) noodles**
2 tablespoons **vegetable oil**
4 **raw king prawns (shrimp)**, peeled and deveined, tails left intact
8 **scallops**, roe removed
75 g (2½ oz/1 cup) shredded **cabbage**
3 **spring onions (scallions)**, cut into 3 cm (1¼ inch) lengths
4 tablespoons **chicken stock** (page 14)
2 tablespoons **chilli jam** (page 109)
1 tablespoon **dark soy sauce**
1 handful **bean sprouts**, trimmed

TO SERVE
1 handful **coriander (cilantro) leaves**
lime wedges

Open up the squid tube and scrub off any soft jelly-like substance, then score the inside of the flesh with a fine crisscross pattern, making sure you do not cut all the way through. Cut the squid into 1 x 2 cm (½ x ¾ inch) pieces. Rinse the hokkien noodles under warm water to separate them, then drain.

Heat the oil in a wok over high heat until smoking. Add the prawns, scallops and squid and stir-fry for 2 minutes, or until the seafood is nearly cooked. Be careful not to overcook the squid or it will become tough. Toss in the cabbage, spring onion and noodles and stir-fry for 2 minutes. Add the stock, chilli jam, soy sauce and bean sprouts and stir-fry for another 1–2 minutes.

Pile the noodles into serving bowls and sprinkle with coriander. Serve with lime wedges.

rice noodles with honey ginger chicken
serves two

3 tablespoons **vegetable oil**
¼ **onion**, sliced
1 **garlic clove**, finely chopped
200 g (7 oz) **boneless, skinless chicken thigh**, thinly sliced
2 **spring onions (scallions)**, cut into 3 cm (1¼ inch) lengths
5 cm (2 inch) piece **fresh ginger**, julienned
1 teaspoon **fish sauce**
1½ tablespoons **light soy sauce**
1 tablespoon **honey**
pinch of **five-spice**
3 tablespoons **chicken stock** (page 14)
1 **long red chilli**, seeded and julienned
250 g (9 oz) **fresh rice sheet noodles**, cut into 2 cm (¾ inch) wide strips

TO SERVE
1 small handful **coriander (cilantro) leaves**
pinch of **freshly ground black pepper**
50 g (1¾ oz/⅓ cup) **roasted cashew nuts**, roughly chopped (page 70)

Heat 2 tablespoons of the oil in a wok over high heat. Add the onion and garlic and stir-fry until fragrant. Add the chicken and stir-fry for 2 minutes, then add the spring onion and ginger and cook for 1 minute. Reduce the heat to medium and add the fish sauce, soy sauce, honey, five-spice, stock and chilli. Cook for 2 minutes, or until the chicken is cooked. Remove from the heat and set aside.

Clean the wok and heat the remaining tablespoon of oil over high heat until smoking. Add the rice noodles and stir-fry for 1–2 minutes, or until the noodles are heated through and are slightly charred but not burnt. Return the chicken mixture to the wok and stir to combine.

Place the noodles and chicken into a serving bowl. Sprinkle with the coriander, pepper and cashew nuts.

char kway teow
serves two to four

2 tablespoons **vegetable oil**
1/4 **onion**, thinly sliced
2 **garlic cloves**, finely chopped
50 g (1 3/4 oz) **boneless, skinless chicken breast**,
thinly sliced
4 **raw king prawns (shrimp)**, peeled and deveined,
tails left intact
6–8 slices **ready-made fish cakes**
50 g (1 3/4 oz) **Chinese barbecued pork (char siu)**,
thinly sliced
2 **eggs**, lightly beaten
250 g (9 oz) **fresh rice sheet noodles**, cut into 1 cm (1/2 inch)
wide strips
1 **spring onion (scallion)**, thinly sliced
1 handful **bean sprouts**, trimmed

SAUCE
1 tablespoon **light soy sauce**
1/2 tablespoon **oyster sauce**
1 tablespoon **dark soy sauce**
pinch of **white pepper**

TO SERVE
1 small **handful coriander (cilantro) leaves**

Combine all the sauce ingredients and set aside.

Heat the oil in a wok over high heat. Add the onion and garlic and stir-fry until fragrant. Add the chicken and prawns and cook for 2 minutes, or until they are nearly cooked. Toss in the fish cakes and pork and stir-fry for 30 seconds.

Pour in the egg, then add the noodles. Stir-fry for 1–2 minutes, or until the noodles soften and the eggs are cooked. Add the spring onion, bean sprouts and sauce and stir-fry for another minute. To serve, pile the noodles into a bowl and garnish with coriander.

HINT _ Ready-made fish cakes can be found in the refrigerator in Asian grocery stores.

rice noodles with beef and black beans   serves two

150 g (5½ oz) **beef rump** or **tenderloin**,
   thinly sliced
3 tablespoons **vegetable oil**
½ small **onion**, thinly sliced
1 **garlic clove**, finely chopped
1 tablespoon **black bean sauce**
2 tablespoons **light soy sauce**
8 **snow peas (mangetout)**, julienned
6 **baby corn**, halved lengthways
3 tablespoons **chicken stock** (page 14)
250 g (9 oz) **fresh rice sheet noodles**, cut
   into 1 cm (½ inch) wide strips

MARINADE
1 tablespoon **dark soy sauce**
1 teaspoon **shaoxing rice wine**
pinch of **sugar**
pinch of **freshly ground black pepper**

TO SERVE
1 **spring onion (scallion)**, thinly sliced
1 small handful **coriander (cilantro) leaves**

Combine all the marinade ingredients in a bowl and stir to dissolve the sugar. Add the beef and toss to coat. Marinate in the refrigerator for 15–20 minutes.

Heat the oil in a wok over high heat. Add the onion and garlic and stir-fry until fragrant. Add the beef and cook for 1 minute. Add the black bean sauce, soy sauce, snow peas, corn and stock and cook for 1–2 minutes. Toss in the noodles and stir-fry until the noodles have absorbed most of the liquid.

To serve, pile the noodles onto a serving plate and garnish with spring onion and coriander.

singapore noodles
serves two to four

150 g (5½ oz) **rice vermicelli noodles**
2 tablespoons **vegetable oil**
1 **garlic clove**, finely chopped
50 g (1¾ oz) **boneless, skinless chicken breast**, thinly sliced into strips
8 **raw prawns (shrimp)**, peeled and deveined, tails left intact
1 large **spring onion (scallion)**, cut into 3 cm (1¼ inch) lengths
50 g (1¾ oz) **Chinese barbecued pork (char siu)**, sliced into thin strips
½ small **onion**, thinly sliced
1 **long red chilli**, seeded and julienned
pinch of **salt**
pinch of **sugar**
2 teaspoons **oyster sauce**
2 teaspoons **mild curry powder**
1 handful **bean sprouts**, trimmed

TO SERVE
1 small handful **coriander (cilantro) leaves**
1 teaspoon **roasted sesame seeds** (page 70)

Soak the vermicelli noodles in cold water for 30 minutes, or until softened. Drain well.

Heat 1 tablespoon of the oil in a wok, add the garlic and stir-fry until fragrant. Add the chicken, prawns and spring onion and stir-fry for 1–2 minutes, or until the chicken and prawns are nearly cooked. Add the pork and stir-fry for 1 minute. Remove and set aside.

Clean the wok and return it to high heat. Add the remaining tablespoon of oil and stir-fry the onion until fragrant. Add the chilli, salt, sugar, oyster sauce, curry powder and 2 tablespoons water, followed by the noodles. Mix well. Toss in the bean sprouts and the prawn, chicken and pork mixture and stir-fry for 1 minute.

To serve, pile the noodles onto a large serving plate, garnish with coriander and sprinkle with sesame seeds.

malaysian rice vermicelli with prawn and garlic chives

serves two

150 g (5½ oz) **rice vermicelli noodles**
vegetable oil, for deep-frying
80 g (2¾ oz) **firm tofu**, cut into thin 2 cm (¾ inch) long strips
12 **raw prawns (shrimp)**, peeled and deveined, tails left intact
30 g (1 oz) **garlic chives**, cut into 3 cm (1¼ inch) lengths
3 tablespoons **chicken stock** (page 14)
1 tablespoon **oyster sauce**
1 tablespoon **dark soy sauce**
1 handful **bean sprouts**, trimmed

PASTE
2 **dried long red chillies**
1 **garlic clove**, peeled
pinch of **salt**

TO SERVE
1 **hard-boiled egg**, quartered
1 small handful **coriander (cilantro) leaves**
1 tablespoon **fried shallots** (page 15)
lime wedges

Soak the vermicelli noodles in cold water for 30 minutes, or until softened. Drain well.

To make the paste, discard the seeds and stems from the dried chillies, then soak in hot water for 10 minutes. Drain, then roughly chop. Using a mortar and pestle, pound the chilli, garlic and salt into a paste. Set aside.

Fill a wok or deep-fat fryer one-third full of oil and heat to 180°C (350°F), or until a cube of bread dropped into the oil browns in 15 seconds. Deep-fry the tofu for 1 minute, or until lightly golden. Drain on paper towels. Clean the wok, reserving 2 tablespoons of the oil.

Heat the reserved oil in the wok and fry the paste until fragrant. Add the prawns and stir-fry for 1 minute. Add the tofu, garlic chives and noodles and stir-fry for another minute. Pour in the stock, oyster sauce and soy sauce and simmer for 30 seconds. Toss in the bean sprouts and stir-fry for a further 30 seconds, or until the prawns are cooked.

To serve, pile the noodles onto a large serving plate. Garnish with the egg, coriander and fried shallots and serve with the lime wedges on the side.

pork bean vermicelli
serves two to four

150 g (5½ oz) **minced (ground) pork**
1 tablespoon **light soy sauce**
120 g (4¼ oz) **bean thread vermicelli (glass)
noodles**
2 tablespoons **vegetable oil**
2 **spring onions (scallions)**, finely chopped

SAUCE
1 tablespoon **chilli bean sauce**
1 tablespoon **light soy sauce**
1 teaspoon grated **fresh ginger**
1 tablespoon **shaoxing rice wine**
125 ml (4 fl oz/½ cup) **chicken stock** (page 14)

TO SERVE
1 small handful **coriander (cilantro) leaves**

Combine the pork with the soy sauce and set aside.

Soak the vermicelli noodles in hot water for 5 minutes. Drain well, then cut into shorter lengths using scissors. Combine the sauce ingredients and mix well. Set aside.

Heat the oil in a wok over high heat until smoking. Add the pork and stir-fry until browned, then add the spring onion and stir-fry for a few seconds. Add the sauce and noodles, reduce the heat to medium and cook for 2–3 minutes, or until the liquid has reduced. Sprinkle with coriander and serve.

bean vermicelli with crabmeat and cloud ear fungus serves two to four

20 g (3/4 oz) **dried cloud ear (black) fungus**
100 g (3 1/2 oz) **bean thread vermicelli (glass) noodles**
2 tablespoons **vegetable oil**
1 **garlic clove**, finely chopped
1 **long red chilli**, seeded and thinly sliced
1 small **carrot**, julienned
2 **spring onions (scallions)**, cut into 3 cm (1 1/4 inch) lengths
1 handful **bean sprouts**, trimmed
250 g (9 oz) **cooked crabmeat**

SAUCE
250 ml (9 fl oz/1 cup) **chicken stock** (page 14)
1 1/2 tablespoons **oyster sauce**
1/2 teaspoon **sesame oil**
1/2 teaspoon **sugar**
1 tablespoon **light soy sauce**
1 tablespoon **shaoxing rice wine**
pinch of **freshly ground black pepper**

TO SERVE
1 small handful **coriander (cilantro) leaves**

Soak the dried fungus in warm water for 20 minutes. Drain and cut into bite-sized pieces, discarding any hard pieces. Soak the vermicelli noodles in hot water for 5 minutes, or until softened. Drain well and cut into shorter lengths using scissors.

Combine the sauce ingredients, stirring to dissolve the sugar. Set aside.

Heat the oil in a wok over high heat until smoking. Add the garlic, chilli, carrot and spring onion and stir-fry until fragrant. Add the fungus and noodles and cook for 1 minute. Add the sauce, bean sprouts and crabmeat. Cook for 1–2 minutes, or until the noodles have absorbed most of the liquid. To serve, pile the noodles into serving bowls and sprinkle with coriander.

rice vermicelli with beef and choy sum
serves two to four

1 tablespoon **shaoxing rice wine**
1 tablespoon **light soy sauce**
pinch of **freshly ground black pepper**
200 g (7 oz) **beef rump**, thinly sliced
150 g (5½ oz) **rice vermicelli noodles**
3 tablespoons **vegetable oil**
2 **eggs**, lightly beaten
100 g (3½ oz) **choy sum**, cut into 5 cm (2 inch) lengths
½ **carrot**, julienned
1 handful **bean sprouts**, trimmed
2 tablespoons **chicken stock** (page 14)
1 tablespoon **oyster sauce**

PASTE
1 **long red chilli**, seeded and chopped
2 **garlic cloves**, crushed
3 **red Asian shallots**, sliced
pinch of **salt**

TO SERVE
1 small handful **coriander (cilantro) leaves**

To make the paste, use a mortar and pestle to pound the chilli, garlic, shallots and salt into a paste. Set aside.

Combine the wine, soy sauce and pepper in a bowl. Add the sliced beef and stir to coat. Leave to marinate in the refrigerator for 30 minutes. Soak the vermicelli noodles in cold water for 30 minutes, or until softened. Drain well.

Heat 1 tablespoon of the oil in a non-stick frying pan. Add the beaten eggs, spreading them evenly over the base of the pan, and cook like an omelette. Cool, then roll the egg up and slice into thin strips. Set aside.

Heat the remaining 2 tablespoons of oil in a wok, add the paste and stir-fry until fragrant. Add the beef and stir-fry for 1 minute. Toss in the choy sum and carrot and cook for 1–2 minutes, or until the choy sum is just cooked. Add the bean sprouts and cook for 1 minute, then add the noodles and stir-fry for another 1 minute. Pour in the stock and oyster sauce and stir-fry until the noodles have absorbed most of the liquid.

Divide the noodles between serving bowls and scatter over the sliced omelette. Garnish with coriander.

hokkien noodles with chicken and shiitake mushrooms serves four

8 **dried shiitake mushrooms**
350 g (12 oz) **boneless, skinless chicken breast**, thinly sliced
3 tablespoons **vegetable oil**
2 **eggs**, lightly beaten
200 g (7 oz) **hokkien (egg) noodles**
1 **garlic clove**, finely chopped
1/2 teaspoon grated **fresh ginger**
2 **spring onions (scallions)**, cut into 3 cm (11/4 inch) lengths
1 **celery stalk**, sliced on the diagonal
1 handful **bean sprouts**, trimmed
2 tablespoons **chicken stock** (page 14)
2 tablespoons **dark soy sauce**
1 small handful **coriander (cilantro) leaves**

MARINADE
1 tablespoon **shaoxing rice wine**
1 tablespoon **light soy sauce**
pinch of **freshly ground black pepper**

Soak the mushrooms in hot water for 20 minutes. Drain, discard the stems and thinly slice the caps. Combine the marinade ingredients in a bowl. Add the sliced chicken and marinate in the refrigerator for 20 minutes.

Heat 1 tablespoon of the oil in a non-stick frying pan. Add the beaten eggs, spreading them evenly over the base of the pan, and cook like an omelette. Cool, then roll the egg up and slice into thin strips. Set aside.

Rinse the hokkien noodles under warm water to separate them, then drain.

Heat the remaining 2 tablespoons of oil in a wok and stir-fry the chicken for 2 minutes. Add the garlic and ginger and stir-fry for 1 minute, or until fragrant. Add the sliced mushrooms, spring onion, celery and bean sprouts and cook for 1 minute, then add the noodles and stir-fry for 1 minute. Add the stock and dark soy sauce and stir-fry until the noodles have absorbed most of the sauce, then stir in the coriander.

Pile the noodles onto a large serving plate and scatter with the shredded omelette.

INDEX

ACKNOWLEDGMENTS

A big thank you to Kay and Juliet for their vision and guidance; Amanda for her encouragement during the process of writing my first book *blue ginger*, and giving me the confidence to write this book; Paul and Kim for their editorial support, and Lauren for her beautiful design; Katy, Ross and Wendy for ensuring all the recipes work and for making the food look delicious; Gorta and Vanessa for their wonderful photography and styling; and to all those people behind the scenes who helped to make this book come together.

Thank you also to my business partner Michael and his wife Paula for their encouragement when I needed it the most; and the team at *Blue Ginger* and *Bar Asia* for their support—I couldn't have done it without you guys .

To my Mum and Dad for their love, support and words of wisdom.

Murdoch Books Australia
Pier 8/9, 23 Hickson Road
Millers Point NSW 2000
Phone: +61 (0) 2 8220 2000, Fax: +61 (0) 2 8220 2558

Published in 2006 by Murdoch Books Pty Limited
www.murdochbooks.com.au

Chief executive: Juliet Rogers
Publishing director: Kay Scarlett

Photographer: Gorta Yuuki
Stylist: Vanessa Austin
Editor: Kim Rowney
Food editor: Katy Holder
Food preparation: Ross Dobson, Wendy Quisumbing
Design manager: Vivien Valk
Design concept and design: Lauren Camilleri
Project manager: Paul McNally
Production: Monika Paratore

Murdoch Books UK Limited
Erico House, 6th Floor North
93–99 Upper Richmond Road, Putney, London SW15 2TG
Phone: +44 (0) 20 8785 5995, Fax: +44 (0) 20 8785 5985

Printed by Midas Printing (Asia) Ltd. in 2006.
PRINTED IN CHINA.

National Library of Australia Cataloguing-in-Publication
Data: Huynh, Leslie, 1968-.
Takeaway: noodle soups, salads and stir-fries
Includes index.
ISBN 978 1 74045 867 2.
ISBN 1 74045 867 2.
1. Cookery, Asian. I. Title. 641.595

CONVERSION GUIDE: You may find cooking times vary depending on the oven you are using. For fan-forced ovens, as a general rule, set the oven temperature to 20°C (35°F) lower than indicated in the recipe. We have used 20 ml (4 teaspoon) tablespoon measures. If you are using a 15 ml (3 teaspoon) tablespoon, for most recipes the difference will not be noticeable. However, for recipes using baking powder, gelatine, bicarbonate of soda (baking soda), small amounts of flour and cornflour (cornstarch), add an extra teaspoon for each tablespoon specified.

The publisher thanks Alex Liddy, Bodum, Dinosaur Designs, Gempoliving, J Style, Love Plates for VNR Australia, Major and Tom, Mao and More, Maxwell & Williams, Mokum Textiles, Mud Australia, Osborne & Little, Papaya, Rhubarb, Robex from Jarass Pty Ltd, Rosenthal Studio Line, Sounds Like Home, and Tomkin Australia for their assistance with the photography for this book.